Coaches, Becoming …

Introduction to 'Coaches, Becoming.'

This anthology contains a variety of individual seasoned coaches' accounts of their experience of 'becoming.' This endeavour was born of a shared curiosity regarding the different start points and directions that they have each found themselves navigating. Through much conversational sharing regarding the 'becoming' process at the Critical Coaching Group, this anthology was born. Each of the narratives are quite different in kind, as befits a highly pluralistic group. It is tempting, as editor, to comment on the whole, but then I find myself resisting that urge, instead allowing the pieces to speak for themselves.

Contributors

Kate Taylor Hewett

Kate has led a portfolio career, lived in an assortment of countries, and enjoys engaging with a kaleidoscope of human thinking, beliefs, emotions and behaviours through the eyes, words and hearts of her coaching clients. She has worked with CEOs, social entrepreneurs, senior healthcare leaders, small company boards, ethical businesses and individuals at career and personal crossroads. Passionate about good leadership and a champion of compassionate, humane systems, she has designed and delivered many leadership development programmes, coaching and communication skills programmes and retreats over the past 18 years, always with the aim of uplifting, cultivating insight and shifting the perspective and habits of everyone involved. She is lucky enough to currently live in the astoundingly beautiful Dartmoor National Park with her husband, an artist and musician, and two somewhat disobedient dogs.

Leslie Goldenberg

Leslie is a coach specializing in leadership transitions. Over the past several years, her work has increasingly come to address the unconscious at work in organizational life. Leslie is currently a student at the Lacanian School of Psychoanalysis of San Francisco. She is also an award-winning ceramic artist. In Leslie's approach, versatility is as essential to coaching as it is to leadership. She blends business acumen, adult development theory, systems thinking, team dynamics, mind-body awareness, and an interest in the unconscious. This includes uncovering knowledge and ideas we don't know we know, and beliefs and assumptions we don't know we have, which offers a way to get beneath the surface of the organizational politics, interpersonal conflicts, and self-limiting patterns that shape our experience. Play is integral to her approach. Word play, role play, and drawing can offer fruitful avenues of insight. Dreams can also be a resource for discerning a truth and a desire of which you have been unconscious.

Martin Vogel

Martin works with leaders and coaches who are exploring how to make a positive impact in these turbulent times. He provides reflective space in which to bring self-knowledge and ecosystemic perspectives to complex challenges. It's a space in which to unknow old certainties, to cultivate self-compassion in the face of difficulty and to allow freshness and creativity to emerge. Martin's approach draws on enquiry skills honed in journalism, coaching and strategy development and a career-long interest in the role of organisations in society. He spent the first half of his career in BBC News where he also initially trained as a coach. He left in 2007 to launch his practice as a counter-consultant, supporting and challenging leaders in media and higher education institutions. He writes about coaching and leadership while exploring ideas around 'unknowing.'

Kay Robinson

Kay is in awe of what happens when we spend time truly connecting with another person, and the power of being seen and heard in a space of acceptance, connecting with our self, with what is important and with what we want – choices become far more straightforward and the path to ease and joy is illuminated. Kay embraces the fact that we are complex systems, with one aspect of our life affecting every part. Kay's career began in the global corporate world where she had her first coaching training, for over twenty years Kay has worked independently with individuals and with groups.

Daniel Doherty

Daniel Doherty is an accidental coach. Coaching as a practice, with a small 'c' has always been around for him, somewhere, from the earliest point, and continues to present itself in many corners of his life to this day. As he has witnessed, over the past few decades, coaching donning the garments of 'professionalism,' while riding a succession of commercial waves, he has critically challenged this new coaching orthodoxy. He remains somewhat in awe of the power of coaching to usher change and transition in people and their organisation systems, while going on his maverick way. Daniel is currently convening writing workshops on the theme of 'becoming' for both coaches and song leaders and writers.

Mary Hughes

I have always preferred work incorporating reflective practice. Coaching training was offered as personal development in the Welsh Public Services, so I accepted and qualified. That was seventeen years ago and it followed a few years of getting acquainted with the profession through managing contracts for coaching services. I then added in-house coaching to my established job, later Action Learning facilitation and wider coaching methods and approaches with experience. When I left the Civil Service, I qualified as a coach supervisor and became an Associate of the University of South Wales as well as being free-lance. I have since coached, supervised, researched, lectured and taught in the field; I continue to do so. Why I love coaching is that it works in the vast, connected complexity of human relations with the many worlds we inhabit. The change that evolves draws on whole lives for adaptations that release it including aspects, once perhaps anathema, of self and the places and ideas of self. That coaching has to be ethical and operate in a place of safety matters to me.

Nickie Bartlett

I've been a doctor for 28 years, mostly working as a consultant in Accident and Emergency with various leadership roles for the last 14years. Six months ago I liberated myself from all my official titled NHS leadership roles. I've been mentoring and coaching formally and informally for about 10 years. Perhaps just as importantly I'm a wife and parent with two grown up children. I'm drawn to patterns and systems, be that the way organisation's function, the way individuals think and behave or how nature creates eco-systems. I've created a forest garden at home and am working with my local hospital to create a forest garden for well-being. I love the systemic thinking that goes with this form of food growing. In my spare time I play in a jazz band, read books and take time to go on long walks in nature, and practice meditation.

Bob Garvey

Bob Garvey is obsessed with coaching and mentoring in all their forms. He is an experienced coach/mentor working with, for example, musicians, HR Managers, small business owners, young people, academics and executives. Bob has great experience in a whole range of different types of organisations. These include large and small businesses, the public and private sector, voluntary organisation and NGOs. He has worked in many different industries including financial services, manufacturing, scientific, creative arts, education and health. Bob subscribes to the 'repertoire' approach to mentoring and coaching. He is in demand internationally as a keynote conference speaker and has published many books and papers on the practice of coaching and mentoring.

Christine Oram

My breadth of experience and depth of expertise informs a keen interest in working with both individuals and organisations to successfully negotiate points of inflection and transformations. With over 20 years' international leadership and programme management experience gained in the not-for-profit sector, I understand acutely the challenges and opportunities you might face when implementing organisational change processes. I have played pivotal roles within the senior management team at a number of major international NGOs, facilitating successful leadership transitions and safely navigating organisational crises. I am driven by expediating the achievement of social justice and bring particular knowledge of human rights, environment, anti-corruption and humanitarian issues.

As Director of Development at Global Witness, I combined an understanding of campaigning and advocacy for social change with my proficiency in strategic programme and financial planning & management; specifically in the development of sustainable funding.

Pippa Warin

Pippa worked for Arts Council England until a couple of years ago, supporting artists of all kinds in ways of making creative ideas real and lasting . She specialises in literature development, working with organisations such as Literature Works, The Lit Platform, Ways with Words and Independent bookshops. One of her earliest projects was producing stories and poems written by women living in refuges in London. More latterly she was the instigator and partnership builder for the successful bid for Exeter to become a UNESCO City of Literature – awarded in Nov 2019 . She enjoys reviewing and mentoring writers and supporting writer events. She is interested in fictional autobiography and perseveres with her own writing in short story / essay form. She is keen on encouraging readership as well as working with creative writers. She has a mentoring and coaching practice , with an emphasis on creative ways of working together.

Jo Cheesman

Jo is compelled to work with others to create a more flourishing future. Her belief is that through embracing the unknowing and uncertainty of our transitional moments, we can together explore new ways to address some of today's complex challenges. She helps others to connect with their purpose, using their agency to bring about positive change.

Through her coaching, she offers light; illuminating new ways to see and make sense of a situation which brings epiphanies. She co-creates a space that is exploratory, reflective and compassionate, allowing for the emergence of something that was not apparent at the outset, the possibility of a different way of being and relating. Prior to focusing on her coaching career, Jo's background has included working in large corporate and public organisations - management consulting, NHS, an international NGO and the Ministry of Defence. She has worked on high-tempo operations, determining responses to global humanitarian crises and international deployments, advising Ministers, with the Cabinet Office, Treasury and FCDO.

Jo is currently engaged in a coaching doctorate, exploring how to change climates, aiming to bring a transdisciplinary approach to create systemic shifts as much as the urgent actions needed for an eco-positive world. Being bold and experimental is deeply enriching her own learning and becoming.

Jeannette Marshall

Jeannette Marshall's journey into coaching was serendipitous. Her inaugural contract occurred in the high-street banking sector, where she was tasked with coaching a challenging cohort of 300 staff. This experience ignited deep introspection, prompting Jeannette to inquire into the foundations of coaching practice. This reflection generated in her insight into the transformative power of coaching. Jeannette's passions include training aspiring coaches and assessors, providing a guiding hand through supervision, and mentoring both novice and seasoned coaching practitioners. For Jeannette, coaching is not simply a profession but a privilege, stamped deep into her personal identity.

. The genesis of this inquiry into coaches' 'becoming.'

This theme of 'coach maturity' within the Critical Coaching Group (CCG,) can be traced back to 2011, later to segue into what we now term coach 'becoming.' This earlier notion of maturity also aligned with ideas at that time as the coach as 'elder.'

It is of little surprise that interest in pursuing this 'becoming' theme has grown as we, the participants and authors of this collection, have ourselves aged. Contemporaneous with this nascent 'becoming' inquiry was the research into 'on the becoming of a coach' - s study led by Professor Bob Garvey of CCG, the findings of which we at CCG have explored in depth with Bob him during several of our 2022/ 23 online and in-the-room CCG gatherings.

Formalising the Becoming Project: scope and purpose

This inquiry became formalised in late 2022. We adopted the term 'becoming' as it aligned with the emergent nature of what we are inquiring into. A principal purpose of this inquiry was to help participants discover something that we each know and cherish about ourselves that we did not know before. This inquiry goes beyond the confines of professional coaching roles, to address the whole person in relationship to the individual's lived life, including their relationship to coaching.

This project is primarily for the benefit of the inquirers, in line with fundamental 'action research' principles. It does not plan to feature classical research outcomes such as peer-reviewed papers or material for conferences that, at times, enhance the researcher above the researched. The primary reason for engaging in action research is 'to assist the actor in improving or refining his or her actions.'

This methodology has been naturalistically driven, and emergent to date. At its heart lies an action research / narrative inquiry / writing-as-inquiry / action learning approach. In spirit, it concerns an inquiry into lived experience, and the process of sense-making from the same inquiry. We have chosen the term 'becoming' with regard to the emergent nature of what we are inquiring into, which is about what we are 'becoming,' and also considers 'how we are becoming.'

This early project formation birthed four regional groups who each set their individual direction, within some broad guidelines and shared time frames. These four groups, based in London, Bristol, Sheffield, and Devon, have met in person, but also online and in a combination of pairs and trios to progress the work. Each regional grouping generated their own 'makings,' including, but not limited to, writing, drawings, diagrams, objects of inspiration, photos, voice recordings, and snatches of jazz, which were collectively shared at the 9 October 2023 gathering.

This gathering generated the identification of 'becoming' themes contained herein. It also provided the inspiration for this group of CCG authors to generate their individual 'becoming' accounts that you now read within this anthology.

Becoming Sky – Kate Taylor Hewett

Wind over Lake: Inner Truth

The old quarry had, over time, been reclaimed by water and encircled by trees. This lake, beneath the eternally changing Devon sky, brought as much character to my early coaching sessions as my human guide. The land held a strong presence behind my foreground mentor, rugged up in a cane chair with his breath misting indivisibly with the vapours of the place. We would watch the rain, ripples or flecks of sunshine play upon the water's surface, listen to birdsong, taste the moist air as it evolved through the seasons. There was a small wood burner in his open-sided hermitage that kept us - mostly – warm, although I would often take advantage of a blanket over my legs to keep my ankles cosy. This was no place for smart casual office gear, shoes had to be ready to meet muddy grass and clothes content to be permeated with woodsmoke. I loved that place, Embercombe, a land-based learning community three miles from my home on the edge of Dartmoor. My mentor read out poems, we shared many moments of silence, and he gently challenged me to uncover what I needed and desired.

That was my way into the potential of coaching. I was running leadership programmes and action learning sets for start-up social entrepreneurs who were full of passion, drive, and often traumatic lived experience of the issues they were attempting to solve. I needed support and the kind of supervision expansive enough to contain my whole life, not just the part of me that functioned in a professional role. I found the simplistic, goal-focussed frameworks common in my field dissatisfying. That is not to say that they were not sometimes useful, but they were often not enough. I was looking for something deeper, for what lurked beneath the visible crust of our human experience.

That longing for the less obvious had deep roots. I had been an ardent student of yoga and meditation for over a decade. I discovered these practices of enquiry into body and mind to be significantly more helpful than anti-depressants when I was living a life I did not love, and that did not love me. Leaving an ostensibly successful technology industry career to become a yoga teacher I had been able to follow this interest for a few years. It was the first significant step I took on the path I am still on today of exploring deeper meaning and continuously challenging my own assumptions about life, work and what it is to be human.

Lake over Wind: Great Preponderance

The idea of me becoming a coach and mentor came from a yoga student. At one point an article was published in the FT Weekend describing a yoga workshop I had run. A woman, who had difficulties travelling to retreats, approached me and asked if I would teach her and her husband at home. She also wondered, as my surname looked familiar, if I might be related to her husband's old university friend. Indeed, the friend was my father, and this thread of synchronicities led me to their home in the Peak district several times a year. The couple were dedicated to their daily practice and struck me as kind, humble and curious folk. I did not see his gentle encouragement to train as a coach as the true compliment it was until I began to read his books and hear so many others speak of how profoundly David Megginson had shaped the coaching and mentoring profession. I stayed with him and his wife Vivien, a sculptor as well as a coach, while studying for the post-graduate qualification in Coaching and Mentoring at Sheffield Business School. Their generosity and Quaker-inspired faith in the good in people provided me with exquisite role modelling.

Wind over flame: Dwelling people

As my coaching practice began to germinate in the compost of the social enterprise sector I was still engaged with, Embercombe catalysed other connections for me in its mycelium-like web. One of these was meeting Simon Western, whose Analytic-Network Coaching system I trained in and who helped me understand how to integrate the 'Soul Guide' discourse I had met in my spiritual studies alongside those I had learned in the business and leadership domains. I also encountered Hetty Einzig again at Embercombe. She had attended my yoga classes for several years although I had not known she was a coach until we both found ourselves at the same Rising Women Rising World weekend. As I grew my network of coaches I began to wonder at the considerable overlap between mindful and embodied practices and coaching. Is the practice of deep listening to others nurtured by deeply listening to ourselves? Or do we begin to listen to ourselves and then wish to share the value we discover with others? It feels no coincidence that yoga, an enquiry into the self, led me to coaching, a joint enquiry into another's self, the life they find themselves in and aspire to create. It also feels no coincidence that a place of natural beauty formed from lake, tree and sky had played a seminal role in this expansion beyond my personal journey. For attending to the wider community of being, to the living exchange of respiration, brings a spaciousness and perspective to our thoughts as well as to our bodies that resounds through all types of practice.

Fire over thunder: Biting through

It had not been my choice to leave yoga teaching for leadership development, but my way had become barred. My body had broken down, its systems had experienced collapse, perhaps not completely but into a tangle where the bramble and nettle had taken over for a while. I had part of my right foot surgically removed due to a rare tumour and could no longer cope with the hours standing on wooden floors that yoga teaching demanded. I needed to return to a desk-based job. So, I found myself starting out again.

Having my body fail brought empathy for others whose health, belief systems, relationships, communities and organisations had done the same to them. It also brought acceptance that our trajectory is rarely linear. I had never understood the five-year career plan, for all my career changes had happened almost by accident, without me knowing what the destination was. Although I persevered with a few yoga classes, and even ran retreats alongside my other work, I stopped teaching completely mid-way through five surgeries related to breast cancer. If there is a rock in the way the tree grows around it. When lightning strikes the tree doesn't give up, it sheds the charred branch and pushes up more life from that which remains alive. As I lived more and more years in the gnarly woods of Dartmoor, I learned to follow the winding paths of instinct over the square boxes of the business matrix, to be guided by my gut upwards to the nourishment of light and downwards to put down roots where nutrients and water can be found. After all, I am not only part of the natural system, I am a natural system.

Wind over earth: Gathering Together

In my life I increasingly saw how our current culture celebrates the individual, and forgets that we are actually communities. This is a new forgetting, as any lineage that goes back more than a few generations has this thinking embedded in its stories. All the yeasts and bacteria, parasites and viruses that live in our guts (and beyond) that we think of as a bit icky but without which we cannot survive are us, too. There is, in fact, more DNA that is 'other' than 'mine' in my body when we include all the billions of bugs. They help us digest the nutrients in our food, they help us maintain immunity. I learned to respect and attend more completely to this biological community in order to regain my health. And yet where do these yeasts and bacteria, parasites and viruses come from? The wider world. We are not isolated, we don't have an impenetrable fence, our skin acts as a fire break to try to protect us, but it is an intelligent barrier that knows, most of the time, what to let in and what to keep out.

This understanding, unsurprisingly, infiltrated my coaching. Instead of seeing myself and my coaching clients as (simply) individuals I learned to view us as intimately and vitally interconnected communities. An organisation is thus a community of communities. Coaching can be a way of acknowledging, creating and maintaining invisible, intelligent boundaries so we can remain healthy in ourselves and contribute to the health of what surrounds us. That involves navigating, with as much skill as we can muster, our human and more-than-human relationships and understanding that the health of this wider community has a profound influence upon our own. Our current human-centred and rationalist culture is a thin (and cracking) veneer over the generations of so-called animists who birthed us. They did not 'believe' that objects and creatures were intrinsically part of the same living word, it was their experience. As children we had no problem believing in talking animals, fish and toys. We can still experience it. Peel off a little more veneer and take a closer look.

Some people may call working with this kind of wider consciousness a systems, ecological or transpersonal approach. The trees use other language, more metaphoric, more sensual, more mythic. If our organisation was a forest, how could we mulch our roots, how might we build the soil for future generations? Would we expect the young sapling swaying in the shade, waiting for the opportunity to shoot up to the overstory, to be as successful as the 400-year-old oak that was there before these times were even a murmur? This is inequality only if we look at the two trees as separate, as not part of the same living system. If we look with a broader lens we see harmony, balance and necessary diversity. How can we admonish the sapling for not trying harder, not working harder, not being sufficiently productive?

Earth over water: Leading

There is no hero's journey in the forest, although it is a place where magic resides. Those who succeed wait, patiently, until the bolt of lightning strikes (what is electricity from the air if not magic?), or the storm comes in on the wake of a full moon, and the old tree falls or drops a branch. Then comes the opportunity to rise that the sapling has been yearning for. Sometimes that opportunity never comes, the ivy climbs up the seedling's waist, the brambles pile on and it is weighed back down to the soil. Sapling becomes mulch. I have had those breaks for the sky, I have had moments of becoming mulch. But nothing can break for the sky without good mulch.

Many of us modern humans may have lost our rooting to place, but we have mobility, creativity and opposable thumbs which means we can travel towards, carry and create opportunities. We are extraordinarily destructive and extraordinary full of love. Holding the expansiveness of sky mind while I speak with clients is a way of bringing this paradox into the conversation. Even a conversation about the tightest, darkest and most limited situation. Ah look, we've almost circled back to something almost spiritual again. Loops and spirals. The shape of the ivy lacing its way up rough bark and the curves of the roots growing around a mossy boulder.

Sky over mountain: Retreat

Today I coach almost entirely via a screen. I see you encased in hard, black, man-made materials with non-negotiable 90-degree corners. Rare are the days when you and I can walk in the woods, or sit on a bench, or at the very least find a window where we might together watch the scudding clouds. Behind me in my Zoom rectangle is a bookcase (full of mythic stories) and a door at a strange angle which leads into a small bathroom. What you cannot see when you are in conversation with me is that just above *your* head, through the rectangles of window above and around my screen, is the same green space of Dartmoor that held me at the beginning of my coaching journey. What you may not know is that the land, sky and more-than-human beings are holding me as I hold you - or perhaps more accurately they are holding us all. I still live only three miles from where it all started. I have chosen to put down roots here, to let this place claim me.

There is an end to each story. But only if we see our stories as separate from all the other stories. This is not a metaphor. This is life. This is what I value and wish to make the most of, and I take a vicarious joy in helping others do the same. Deepening my capacity to co-experience the grief and the joys of those I work with, to meander with purpose through the beauty of the thinking process, to honour the stories that need to be told is, for me, a sign of becoming. When I become lake and you become tree, we are both able to behold the awesome beauty of sky.

Becoming Coach - Leslie Goldenberg.

Several years ago I had a dream of being at the edge of a cliff. In the dream, I hear a voice saying, "don't back up" in a very directive tone. My position in the dream is unclear. Am I facing the open air beyond the edge of the cliff, or am I facing the safety of the land? If I back up, would I go over the edge and tumble into the abyss, or would I back up onto firm ground? I am also uncertain about the identity and source of the voice. It's a presence more than a person.

This simple dream has been insistent in my recall, and I have worked with it a great deal, seeking to understand its unconscious wishes and enigmatic meanings. I dreamt it shortly after the death of Pat Adson, an influential coach in the institute where I originally trained, who died several years ago in her 90's. A colleague visited Pat's deathbed and asked what final wisdom she wanted to impart. Pat's words were, "don't wait," a message that touched this visiting colleague and prompted her to convey Pat's final words to many others. One interpretation is that the dream was a sort of echo, a slight transformation and specification of Pat's message. Another interpretation is a wish to stay at the edge, neither backing up over the brink nor moving onto safer ground.

Staying at the edge is also a metaphor for remaining on the fringe rather than the middle of things, which makes me think of Kurt Vonnegut's saying that you can see more from the edge than from the centre. The interpretations and associations can go on and on.

I have found myself in many different landscapes looking over the edge of a cliff and thinking of this dream again and again. The echoes continue. The invitation to write this reflection was yet another one, this time an invitation to create a 'cliff narrative' about the formation of coaching identity. How has becoming a coach been a way of staying at the edge?

When people ask me questions about the beginnings of becoming a coach - "How long have you been a coach?" or "When did you start coaching?" - I answer that there are two ways of seeing it. One is the origin story of the professional path, and the other is the personal formation.
Professionally, I was a consultant who performed strategy studies and offered support in the implementation of new strategies. I gravitated to the part of the work that involved dialogue with client leaders about the role of their own behaviour and mindset in making change happen in their organizations. I got into designing and facilitating experiential learning events in support of this and eventually moved into

executive coaching because I enjoyed working with people one-on-one more than with teams or larger groups.

To prepare for a coaching credential, I studied at the Hudson Institute, a program that includes a substantial grounding in psychological and developmental theories. In the succeeding years, many other formal training programs have added layers to the Hudson foundation. Offerings from unconventional sources have been a source of great influence. For example, I completed a program in becoming a death doula, centring on the study of conscious dying and deepening my appreciation for, and practical knowledge about, ways of working with the ultimate transition, the ever-present ending, the final cliff.

My encounter with Lacanian psychoanalysis is another unconventional strand which continues to shape the coach I am becoming. Lacan famously reinterpreted a quote from Freud, which in German would be *"woe es var, soll ich werden,"* often translated as "where it was, there shall I be" and which Lacan interpreted as "where it was, I shall be becoming." I take this to mean that there is something about that "it," that force in our life, that helps us or insists in us or requires us to keep becoming. My encounter with these ideas began with a book by Annie Rogers, which led to a personal analysis, which led to attending years of seminars, and now I find myself hosting a seminar, giving talks about Lacan and coaching, becoming a candidate at a school of Lacanian psychoanalysis, and describing myself as an analytic coach.

In addition to professional strands of becoming, there are also personal ones. I grew up in a household with a brother who was troubled from a very young age. The word used to describe him back then was 'rambunctious.' He had a high IQ, a learning disability that impaired his ability to write, and an emotional volatility that unpredictably erupted in hostile aggressivity. In today's world he might have been diagnosed with ADHD or oppositional disorder or some combination. There was a lot of family therapy and various forms of accommodation for my brother, many of which didn't make sense to me, or felt unjust to me, penalized me, limited me. And so, I was frequently asking, why are we doing things this way? Do we have to do things this way? I think these are fundamental coaching questions about the reason why things are the way they are, and to ask, are there other possibilities?

Fear of my brother's fury had great power in the household. The prime directive was "don't provoke him and don't let him provoke you." The firm installation of these words in my psyche shaped me profoundly. I learned all sorts of ways to enjoy provoking him on the sly, my favourite being the silent treatment. I also learned all sorts of ways to maintain equanimity amidst chaos. Even with years of reflective practices to shed light on and undo some of this unconscious patterning, I am certain that this history continues to shape my identity and thus colour the way I work as a coach.

The recognition of becoming a coach from the very beginning as a role in the household didn't occur to me until relatively recently. As Kierkegaard says, we live our lives forward, and make sense of them backwards.

Taking up a coach-like role in the household was a response not only to my brother, but also to my parents. My father was an alcoholic and a gambling addict - - fun, affectionate, hedonistic - - and also quite troubled. My mother was a very unusual woman, a pioneer for her era, one of the first women in the engineering profession. She specialized in HVAC systems for high rise buildings. She had many of the stereotypical engineer qualities. She was brilliant, a concrete thinker, aloof, and had very little attunement or natural human connection capability. She had no friends, and very little EQ. If she were a child in school today, she would probably be considered on the spectrum. I am proud of my mother and learned a great deal from her about being a professional woman, but as a kid, I was always looking for surrogate mothers, for surrogate mothering, and fortunately I found what I needed in many places. Perhaps I was drawn into coaching as a way of becoming that surrogate myself, trying to see and hear others in ways I always longed to be seen and heard.

Another strand that stands out in my becoming coach is my work as an RA, a Resident Assistant, in the university dormitories. It's a role as peer leader that includes a kind of coaching. Have you heard that there is an epidemic of mental health issues and emotional distress on university campuses? My experience suggests that this is not a new phenomenon. In the 1980's, residents in my building would come to my room to sit on my couch, (literally, I did have a couch), and talk to me about all kinds of things. My RA training included the first instruction I'd ever received in how to listen and ask open questions and make referrals. This was the start of becoming more skilful in these foundational acts of coaching.

Questions about the origins of becoming a coach braid these and so many other strands together. I'm still, and always will be, in the process of becoming coach. These days, I see the process of becoming coach entangled with becoming artist, and becoming more of who I am in all kinds of ways, and finding ways to name what I am.

I have a great deal of trouble with the word 'coach.' It has come to be a signifier that says something, to generate an assumed meaning, but it doesn't say what I want it to say. It doesn't say enough. Or maybe it says too much. But it says something that's recognizable that other people can hang their associations onto. When I say what I actually like to say, it feels good coming out of my mouth: I have an analytic studio, a space where things happen, and where we can create. No one knows what an analytic studio is. It sounds like maybe I'm a kind of drama teacher. And perhaps that's partly true. I've been using more and more techniques from psychodrama in my coaching and the man in my life is a gifted practitioner of psychodrama.

I've also been inviting dreamwork into my coaching practice. I have been interested in my dreams for decades, ever since an early therapist encouraged me to pay attention to them. This question of becoming coach and what it means to coach or to be a coach has been showing up in my dreams. I've had several dreams about trains and train stations. Of course, trains are made up of coaches. I've dreamed about jumping the tracks. I wonder about all of these meanings and associations. There are a lot of other things going on in the coaches and train stations in these dreams, and many layers and interpretations to consider.

In addition to working with my own dreams, I have invited some of my clients to pay attention to their dreams and speak about them, and they tell me that's been interesting and fruitful for them.

Dreams arise from the realm of the unconscious. Christopher Bollas offers a way of thinking about the unconscious as 'the unthought known' - - something we know enough about to dream, but haven't brought to conscious thought. I'm convinced that there is a great deal to be gained by attending to the unknown, to honor, trust, and make space for what is unknown and unconscious. Or am I going over the cliff here? Is dreamwork suitable domain for someone who still calls herself a coach?

If something is becoming to you, it means that it looks good on you. Is being a coach becoming to me? Does it become me to be a coach?

Contemplations on becoming a mature coach – Martin Vogel.

What is the price of Experience? Do men buy it for a song? Or wisdom for a dance in the street? No, it is bought with the price Of all that a man hath.
– William Blake, *Songs of Innocence and Experience*

1)

What does it mean to be a mature coach? A question posed by my participation in the Critical Coaching Group's "becoming" project.

The notion of becoming evolved out of the group's explorations of coach maturity. But becoming and maturity are not equivalents.

Maturity suggests arrival, the possession of wisdom – acquired, as Blake attests, at some cost.

Becoming suggests transition and speaks perhaps not to maturity but to ageing.

Some of us in the CCG's discussions have reached a life stage where moving on from a full working life is on the agenda.

But moving on to what?

These questions of maturity and becoming are pertinent for me, having recently reached my sixties.

Enjoying the maturity of my practice, I nonetheless contemplate whether, when and how to draw my professional coaching life to a close.

This raises the possibility of becoming, of course – a transition to something new. But, more pertinently, there is unbecoming.
A hesitance to let go inhibits my becoming.
What am I, if I am ceasing to be a coach?

1

2)

Becoming a coach in the first place was an act of maturation.

I came to coaching having been a journalist.

My development as a coach, in middle age, was a synthesising of life experience with new skills in pursuit of a practice of service and entrepreneurship.

Entrepreneurship is a self-aggrandising term for the business-building that accompanied the unfolding of my professional practice.

"Wisdom," said Blake, "Is sold in the desolate market where none come to buy." I certainly paid my dues in that place.

Through 16 or 17 years' practice, my professional identity was that of a coach becoming – always in development, never arriving.

Then something changed and I began to notice the exit.

During the Covid lockdowns, I began to feel disconnected from the coaching profession and the professional questions it was addressing through CPD workshops, courses and articles.

To some extent this was a reflection of prospective retirement, however distant, and a consequent diminishment in the impetus for continuing professional development.

But I was also feeling that CPD, and the attendant debates in the profession, were not meeting my needs as a mature practitioner.

Maturity can signify a harvesting of wisdom, but it can also signify ossification. Perhaps both these dimensions were present in my disposition.
I was noticing a confidence in my intuitions and instincts, borne of experience.

I was also feeling that the broader social and political currents that inform debates around coaching were reflecting the preferences of a younger generation, and perhaps it was time for me to step aside.

2

If you recall that some of the debates that came to the fore around this time concerned climate change, racial equity and gender identity, you should not read into this any particular interpretation of where I stand on these issues.

What I was detaching from was the stridency with which colleagues in the coaching community – and indeed the wider corporate world – were colluding with new and only partially thought through orthodoxies.

My professional practice champions resistance to received thinking and advocates space for thinking through questions for oneself.

If this space was closing down in the supply and demand for coaching, I wondered how much longer this would be a profession in which I could thrive.

3)

The Critical Coaching Group – described by its convenor, Daniel Doherty, as a confederacy of mavericks – provided a forum in which I could continue to pursue professional development while indulging a sceptic mien.

Their exploration of maturity and becoming, at just the time when I was questioning my path, addressed my need for a deeper, more expansive developmental enquiry.

Among the words that reverberate in our conversations are scepticism, prodding, provoking, curiosity, challenge, enquiry, transgression, iconoclasm, non- conformism.

There is also a collective identity of being practitioners at the top of our game.

This is the territory of maturity and it resonates with me.

To a point.

Implicit in the construct of maturity is a conviction that one has reached a degree of mastery and can settle into a more fluid, spontaneous style of practice.

I indulged in believing this of myself for a while.
But I find mastery to be a dangerous and self-deluding bauble.

3

It poses great risk to a practitioner if it induces a suspension of (self-)critical thinking.

The moment of greatest knowing is when we become most oblivious to our blind spots.

If I had reached a point of self-proclaimed mastery, this was surely another signal that my useful life as a coaching practitioner is nearly spent.

This is a contradiction of my maturity as a coach: the completion of becoming contains the beginning of a new unbecoming.

4)

In retrospect, my whole becoming as a coach was an act of unbecoming.

Not only did this entail the unravelling of the identifications of my previous career but of the constructs of coaching that I brought into my initial formation and those I acquired further along the way.

To begin with, I bought into stuff about goals, plans and solutions.

They reflected my belief in a world that was manageable and susceptible to well- intentioned human intervention.

Nowadays, I hold these ideas lightly if at all – dispelled by years of mendacious leadership, political chaos and inertia on climate and biodiversity.

Also along the way, I have integrated ideas from other domains about which I am now more sceptical.

These include mindfulness, psychodynamics, critical theory.

On the other hand, a constant through my working life has been an attachment to story.

Our drive to narrate believable stories seems to me to be core to how we structure reality and make sense of a complex and sometimes disorderly world.

Beyond cognitive sense-making, telling and witnessing stories are acts of social connection and thus emotional and existential validation.

4

It is the relational act of storytelling that gives coaching meaning.

My facility with this dimension of my practice is not something I will let go, however my commitment to being a coach evolves.

In our collective reflections in the Critical Coaching Group, we have wondered if maturity might be viewed as the reaching of a terminal point in one's professional development.

I find this a relevant insight.

No longer becoming a coach, I am a mature coach.

Yet still becoming.

While unbecoming.

If my earlier drive to acquire development as a coaching practitioner has diminished, this does not signal an end to development per se but a shift of focus.

I'm drawn to a post-coaching existence that doesn't eliminate coaching from my life but integrates it in a looser way.

My desire to work as a coach is balanced by an awareness of unfinished business in other parts of my life to which I want to attend as I enter my Third Act.

The gifts that coaching can offer have always struck me as too narrowly distributed. And not just that.

Insofar as coaching functions as part of the repertoire of corporate life, I find it has insufficient impact on the values and practices of corporates.

Organisations are best construed as artificial intelligences impervious to the ministering of a peripatetic professional coach.

Coaches might earn a living through them but they can have more impact on the world by conducting their practice elsewhere.

It is this pursuit of impact that interests me now, admittedly because the exigencies of earning a living are less pressing at this stage of life.

It turns out that maturity is a function of economics as much as experience.

5

The Language of the Soul - Kay Robinson

It's a golden August morning, on the day that I notice I'm alive.
Early light seeps through the curtains, I make plans, noting all
I need to do to take my excited boys to the beach. I move to
get out of bed and as I try to stand, my legs buckle beneath
me. It feels surreal, distant. Not happening to me.
I become a powerless mass on the floor.
Hours later, I'm in the cardiac unit of our local hospital, my
body covered in sensors and connected to various machines.
I've learned a new term, heart failure. The doctor's face,
intently serious, a slight shake of his head as he feels my
pulse. I'm a tall, strongly built, forty-four-year-old, alongside
my fragile elderly wardmates, I feel like an animal in the wrong
cage at a zoo.
'Stop,' says my body.
I am stopped. Virtually strapped to the bed.
Absent are the chaotic demands of children, injured husband,
dogs, elderly parents, setting up a coaching business, …….
There are no answers to why I am here.
I rest, without choice, waiting for each day to unfold.

***

My thoughts drift to another rude awakening, years ago.
I struggle to open my eyes. Apparently, my eyelids are
weighted down and lined with gravel. My mouth and throat are

so dry, I cannot swallow. A small relief, there is the comfortable spring of a bed beneath me. I am bewildered by the restriction of clothes and the weight of my long winter coat. Knees bent, my feet are on the floor, encased in high heeled boots. In the dim light, I slowly turn my head and realise I am in a hotel room, my suitcase is parked near the desk. Catching sight of it triggers a set of realisations and questions that send me into a sudden frenzied state of uncoordinated action.

On my feet. Hot. Spine dripping. Where am I? What day is it? Is it day or night? Which country? City? Which hotel? Did I miss a meeting? Where should I be right now?

Sleeping is definitely not part of my itinerary; I am flooded with guilt. My legs almost give way as I stand and scan the room for my rucksack. My executive rucksack, to which I am unreasonably attached. It is my constant companion as I travel the world, it contains all that I need to connect and communicate with others. All that I need to work, to be efficient, to be effective, to 'perform'. As I look down, I almost faint with relief as I realise, I am standing right next to it. Several minutes later, I am breathing easily, resting my tired body and allowing my brain to become fully awake and functioning again. I am in New York, in a Hilton hotel in Manhattan. It is Sunday evening local time. I have a meeting on Monday morning. Relief permeates my body. There is no need to rush around.

I remember my flight from London, following a hurried twenty-two hours at home. A pit-stop. Time for transition, to unpack, re-equip and repack. Call my mother and snatch a few, too few, hours with my husband. I remember the light, the sounds, the faces, the many many faces and the heat from the days of my trip to Mumbai, barely 48 hours ago.

Water, that most basic of elements is my saviour. Cool and infinitely delicious it slips down my dry throat, eases my muzzy head and rehydrates my body. Hot and fast flowing in the shower it soothes my aching muscles and washes away the dirt, sweat and fatigue of travel. As my body is cleansed and refreshed, I become aware of a shift at the core of my being, a decision has been made.

There is an unfamiliar sense of wholeness and completion within me, a certainty of what is right and what I want. I'm about to leave the tyrannous luxury of my corporate life, make my ninth house move in fourteen years, to a place and a house of my choosing, back to rural life, to a home, where we will live for more than twenty years.

***

I think back to how in earlier times I was eager and chafing for challenge.

With the sky is a distant pale grey and the wind not too strong, we're above the low-lying office block and the local buildings. We ignore the far-reaching views, being intent upon gazing

44

into the dark interior of a storage tank. The odour is unpleasant.

'So, what d' you think? How much is in there?' My companion asks in his deep northern voice, large nicotine-stained teeth exposed. He can't stop himself grinning.

'I haven't a clue. What d'you think?' I look him straight in the eye, serious, but enjoying his sense of humour.

He gives a non-committal grunt, and gently lays a restraining hand on my arm, as I move to lift my safety goggles trying to get a better look, 'You mustn't do that.'

We climb back down the long metal ladder, my feet in unfamiliar safety boots, new, like my white coat and shiny yellow hard hat. My companion leads the way, we are stock-taking at a chemical plant. He is over sixty years old and has worked here for more than forty years. As we walk and talk, we realise he had already been working here for fifteen years, at the time I was born. He shows me round the site while we measure, count and record.

He is one of my three, middle-aged, assistant managers, who each have several clerks working under them. And if my language is archaic, it was the 1990s. Yes, I'm his boss. How does life work, that at twenty-five, I'm the one held responsible, rather than those who've worked here for decades?

I was lucky. Born to a life where I could go to university, be accepted onto the graduate development scheme of a blue-chip multinational, pass my finance exams to become a chartered management accountant, whilst being shuttled around various departments for a couple of years. So, obviously, I'm the one qualified to be in charge.

Painfully aware of my youth and inexperience, I unconsciously follow my father's example, from years of observing him drawing out in conversation the visitors to our lively household, asking questions and listening with gentle curiosity and respect. I learn that people learn as they explain, as they seek to find means to layout a problem, to make it clear, they gain clarity themselves, the solution becomes obvious. They know what to do and all I do is listen and ask what I hope are intelligent questions.

My style of management, or is it leadership, is set. I feel like I've found a cunning trick, it makes work easy; and I enjoy the relationships we create.

***

My wakeful dozing is interrupted by the familiar irregular rhythm of two pairs of crutches.

My parents arrive breathless and exhausted, at my bedside. They look more at home here than I do. Their grim faces become less taut as I rouse myself to be alert and conversational. I have no news to soften the reality of my state, the doctors are baffled, I have no risk factors and the tests have shown almost nothing.

Once they leave, we indulge our separate but mutual worries. I, picturing their painful, slow progress through long hospital corridors; they, baffled, conjecturing, what possible reason can there be for my heart to suddenly slow down? What about the children?

And perhaps it is as well that none of us know what lies ahead.

My parents live to know that I recover from this bout of myocarditis, my heart inflamed, reacting to a virus; that blood tests showing elevated calcium, lead to the discovery of parathyroid tumours in my neck; that I recover from throat surgery to remove the tumours and return to normal life; that we lose my father-in-law, ten years their junior, within months of his diagnosis.

My parents do not know that they will both suffer horrible deaths, just over a year apart, or that I will become familiar not only with Cardiology, but also Oncology and Haematology. They do not know how much I miss them as I experience cancer treatments, or how glad I am that they do not have to bear witness.

They do not know of my eldest son's illness that prevents him living a normal life from the age of fourteen, how much I miss their support, or of our grief for his misplaced years.

Almost ten years of illness and loss, leave me feeling as though I've been carried out to sea into the darkness of a perpetual storm, repeatedly hurled against jagged rocks until I'm broken into pieces, which lie shuddering with absent life.

My coaching clients deserve better.

Having tried many therapies, both mind and body, this time I seek help from another coach. Fascinated by the concept of clean language I had heard about when studying Neuro Linguistic Programming, I look for a clean coach and find Annemiek van Helsdingen running the Soul-based coaching Academy from the Netherlands. I am so ready for change. Is that my soul I hear screaming?

***

'And there's a part of you that is angry. And that part that's angry. Where is that?' Annemiek, looks at me intently from her home in the Netherlands, she has found an area of tension she wants to bring to my attention.

My thoughts scatter and reform. Such an odd question. How do I know? How am I supposed to find an answer? I glance at the screen, Annemiek is sitting waiting, expecting, waiting. I close my eyes and focus on my body and on the feeling of anger.

'I think it's in my abdomen, sort of deep, low down. I don't know how to describe it.' Is my eventual reply after several minutes when Annemiek has stayed silent, giving me time to tune in, to connect to myself.

'And it's in your abdomen deep and low down. Does it have a size or shape?'

'It has a texture and it's hard.'

'It's hard. And does it have a colour?'

'It's dark'

'It's dark and hard. And how big is it, that hard, dark in your abdomen?'

I keep my eyes closed, focusing, listening to Annemiek's voice, looking for answers to her questions. I am too focused and absorbed to consider how weird it is to find something hard and dark in my abdomen.

'It's, it's not that big. It's like a walnut with a shell.'

'Like a walnut with a shell, hard and dark and deep in your abdomen low down. Is there anything else about that deep dark walnut with a shell?'

'It's like it's been stored. In a warehouse and there are things that come and go, it's a busy warehouse. In a dark corner there's something that's just sat there and sat there and sat there and nobody's come to get it or take it away it's just stayed rather than being part of this dynamic movement of the warehouse.'

'And what would that walnut like to have happen when it's been stored in this deep dark place?'

'I don't know what it wants, what I want is for it to go.'

The walls are painted a perfect white, the floor is a gleaming grey. The racks are six metres tall with deep accommodating shelves. Bright fluorescent light illuminates the scene. At the entrance, there is a sense of calm efficiency and purpose. Goods are moving in and out as required, with just-in-time ease.

A fluorescent light in a far corner begins to flicker and extinguish. The corner is almost dark, on a shelf at waist height there is a small metal box, like an old-fashioned cash box.

'And you'd like it to go, and it's been there for a long time, and it hasn't moved.'

Both the shelf and the box are thick with dust. I instinctively know this box will be heavy and hard to move, almost welded to the shelf. The dark and the dust are contaminating the pristine warehouse.

'And you would like it to go?'

'If I move it will the shelves collapse? Will the warehouse be destroyed?' I'm finding it hard to speak, Annemiek is watching me intently, waiting for me to respond.

'What's happening now?' Annemiek checks in with me, bringing me back to remember I'm in a coaching session. 'What would it be like in my body if the hardness was gone that hard sort of lump and what would it be like in the warehouse? If it wasn't there? What would I do with that shelf? Could I put the lights on in that corner?'

'What kind of lights are there in the warehouse?'

'I could turn the lights on in the corner to clear out what isn't moving. How any business does, go through and get rid of old stuff they don't need. The old-fashioned dark box, it's not up to date with all the different labels.'

'That is the box, the old-fashioned box, with the labels not updated and you think it's heavy or difficult to move? And you're worried you might upset the balance of the shelving when you do. What would the old-fashioned old box like to have happen when it's not been updated?'

'It feels out of place in a modern warehouse, like it's been forgotten.'

'It feels like it's been forgotten.'

'Neglected.'

'It feels like it's been neglected. And what would it like to have happen when it feels like it's been neglected?'

I am curious to see what is in the box, why does it get a whole shelf, this small box. Why is it still here. I am peering at it through the gloom, I can't see it clearly. On impulse I decide to move the box to the entrance and into the bright light, to see it more clearly.

As I make that decision there is a physical eruption within my body, as though something is being expelled at extreme velocity. I am thrown forward and sideways on my chair. There is a lump in my throat, panic, panic, it will stop me breathing, swallowing. Suddenly it's gone. I have disappeared from the screen. Annemiek calls me back.

'Sit on your chair, put your feet on the ground, look at me, breathe.'

I take a moment to catch my breath.

'Is the lump not there?'

'It's as If it's evaporating,'

'And it's as if it's evaporating. And where are you now? When the lump Is evaporating'

'I'm nowhere. I'm not in the warehouse. The black box is just a memory. It's like moving it has created an eruption which is almost like a black hole.'

'Eruption into a black hole. That's what moving it was. And what went into the black hole?'

'Everything in the warehouse. The whole thing and me'

'Everything went into the black hole. And you. And what would you like to have happen?'

'My body is readjusting. Something's changed.'

'What is it that's changed?'

'It's like my body is adjusting to the fact that something's just driven through it.'

'And what happens to you when your body is adjusting to that?'

'Well, I am my body, isn't it the same thing?'

'And when you're adjusting, and your body is adjusting What would you like to have happen now?'

'To let it happen, let the adjustment happen. Let it re-organise, it will end up in the right place.'

In the days following this session, I decide not to attempt to rationalise or analyse my experience. I don't even want to know what was in the box, it is gone and that is enough. I feel an intense lack of anxiety. I am grounded in the present, as though my brain is busy elsewhere. I am almost stuck in the present and I begin to find it claustrophobic. Relief comes a few days later when my brain returns to flitting as usual.

Clean questions were developed by David Grove, a New Zealand psychotherapist, who noticed that client's descriptions of their trauma often included metaphors and when he asked questions about their metaphors (rather than the trauma itself), without contaminating or distorting them, it helped them to change their perception of the trauma and to heal.

David Grove's approach was modelled by Penny Tompkins and James Lawley. They spent hours observing him with clients, analysing transcripts of his sessions to understand his work and find patterns that could be replicated; testing and fine-tuning, until they had a model they called Symbolic Modelling which they could use to teach others and to use the principles in other contexts, such as coaching.

This technique embraces the fact that our brains use metaphor from our earliest days, we locate the concepts we learn about. We unconsciously experience and think about one thing in terms of another – each of us creating our own unique metaphors to comprehend the world. Our everyday language and internal dialogue is littered with metaphor. Understanding and becoming aware of our metaphors allows us to access our deepest knowing, they are the language of our souls, of our subconscious minds and of our bodies. Accessing our metaphors and identifying what we want, can help us re-wire our subconscious minds. There is no need to translate our metaphors, or relate them to the rest of our lives, a change in a metaphor dreamscape, replicates in normal life.

***

Eighteen months from starting my soul-based coaching sessions using symbolic modelling, my journal reads:

I am alive. My whole-body fizzes with excitement, I am revelling in life. It is glorious. I celebrate all that life is and that I am part of it.

A few months into my work as a client, I begin the year-long training, learning to facilitate my own coaching clients using metaphor. This is not just another tool for my toolbox. Being able to help clients access the power and creativity of their subconscious minds, it feels like I've found another cunning trick, a shortcut to magic, working with their minds and the embodiment of their truth.

And in a world where we are elusive even to ourselves, I learn to trust myself to feel the pain I've hidden, to allow it to process and flow through my body. I learn to notice when I need to remember I'm alive, to connect to inner stillness, and to be calm enough to listen to the voice that always knows. I know that my work in a space that becomes sacred, with human connection and transformation, is exactly where I'm meant to be.

Musings on becoming – Nickie Bartlett

"Entomology of WEIRD: Old English wyrd 'Destiny' of Germanic origin. The adjective (Late middle English) originally meant 'Having the power to control destiny' and was used especially in the Weird Sisters, originally referring to the Fates, later the witches in Shakespeare's Macbeth; the latter gave rise to the sense of 'Unearthly.'"

It took me a while to decide how to approach this piece of writing. I could write a chronology of happenings and experiences that have shaped who I am and how I coach, but somehow that doesn't capture the inner workings of 'Becoming.' I've tried to extract my 'Becoming' as a coach from my 'Becoming' as a human being. I can't, they're inextricably linked, meshed in a tangled mess. So here are a few musings. Random stuff that I think about, experiment with and explore. In my world it's all connected.

I love that place where science, mythology and spirituality meet. It feels like a place of alchemy. It's a coalescence where gateways open inside and outside, for all things to enter and exit. It feels earthy, and sometimes putrid with overtones of magic. It's a place of exploration, adventure, distillation and sometimes trepidation. Much of what is here written sits in that place of joining.

Truth

"Whoever undertakes to set himself up as judge of Truth and Knowledge is shipwrecked by the laughter of Gods." Einstein

Once upon a time, what I saw and what I heard and interpreted was a firm foundation for Truth. I lived in this world with a firm footing, an assurance that everything was as it seemed. I didn't notice that I didn't notice things that were just out of vision. Well, you don't, until you do…then life gets a whole lot more complicated and a whole lot more interesting. I couldn't wear blinkers anymore, no more myopic glasses. Instead, I opened myself up to the possibility of other possibilities…like my truth might not be somebody else's truth. My truth was almost certainly not my daughter's truth and sometimes it wasn't even my husband's truth. That can be a bit problematic! But, what a joy to entertain the idea that the world was full of alternatives, different ways, different paths. There are times when I hear other people's truths when I feel an empty aching in my chest, a longing to open myself wide to the experience of others and just 'be' alongside. I sometimes feel grief for the contradictory truths of humanity.

Failing

"The wound is the place where the Light enters you." Rumi

If anybody tells me again, that it's ok to fail at stuff because it's all learning…I am going to shout very loudly and stamp my feet like a toddler and generally get very angry. I know it's true, but let's be honest, it's ok to be pissed off, angry and upset by failing. When I'm not coaching, I am doctoring. When I make a mistake, a misjudgement and a patient comes to harm, I feel sick. I sometimes go through a period of feeling terrible self-doubt and on occasion I have experienced days of dissociation. The old adage, 'Don't worry…nobody's died', doesn't really apply. You see the consequences of my failings aren't just felt by me. There's a ripple effect with the patient, another human being, at the centre, and that really matters to me. Yes, I will learn, I will become more human, more forgiving of myself and in turn, those around me. But I need to be angry and upset first. That needs to be ok, for a bit.

Then there's all the leadership work…well that's a minefield. There were times when it was difficult for me to know whether I was failing or succeeding, and that's probably too binary anyway. It's likely I was failing and succeeding at the same time, depending on what front was being looked at and who was being asked, what was being measured, who was doing the measuring and who was interpreting the results. Some important stuff is hard to measure anyway. I learned to live with these shifting sands and listen to extraneous chatter with a discerning ear. Sometimes it was important to let things fail. A kind of deliberate failing that might be used as a lever for subsequent success. Was that my failing, or maybe that was my success, who knows? Nothing is linear, it's not even nicely interwoven simple circles. It's more like the undergrowth in a wood with hundreds of interconnections and interdependencies. It was all so grey, a big boggy quagmire with a perpetual heavy fog hanging over it. Often it felt like I was groping about in the grey, and an occasional sunbeam shone through which I grabbed, and then it would slip away, or a lightning bolt would come sideways and shatter it into a thousand pieces. It wasn't always like that though. In more recent times I found I could make things happen, difficult stuff became easier as self-belief grew while paradoxically, the need to prop up my ego faded. But still those lightning bolts came.

I wonder whether leadership is just a process of learning how to cope with failing whilst maintaining some sort of semblance of hope. And hope, was that for me or to keep those going around me? Both I guess. Hope with eyes open, looking out and looking in and searching. There were times when I needed a very big and bright search light to find hope.

Stories

"Fiction, not truth, is what we humankind live in, and truth arises from fiction, not the other way round." Lydia Fakundiny and Joyce Elbrecht

I am shaped by the stories I tell about myself and the world I inhabit. But these stories have evolved and shifted over time. The stories I held of my childhood, particularly through my lens as a teenager have been retold with a grown-up lens. A new lens shaped by parenting teenagers myself. Does that make them any closer to the truth…I doubt it, but it makes them different, less angsty! The stories I tell myself about the death of my mother have been re-examined, retold, scrutinised again, checked with my sister and retold again. The story that she is 'Gone' has been thrown away. Of course, she is still with me. She is present all the time in my memory, in my heart and in my being. My children know her, they just haven't met her, she will always be with us.

An elderly Irish lady who performed a Tarot reading for me, told me that my Mum sits next to me in the car when nobody occupies the passenger seat. That set me wondering what Mum thinks about my little Mini. When she was alive in this world, she seemed quite a conventional woman to me…a primary teacher who ran the local Brownie company and led the church choir. But then again, she drove a bright yellow two-seater Triumph Spitfire, at what felt like breakneck speed around the little lanes where we lived, sometimes with the roof down. People have layers that sometimes break through, that we sometimes glimpse, but stay hidden most of the time.

Divination…now that's a thing.

Music
"Music is indeed the mediator between the spiritual and sensual life." Ludwig van Beethoven

Music has been a big part of my life since I was a child. Playing music has been my inspiration and my therapy. Music tells stories. Folk music seems to contain its own musical genetic code. It passes like a meme from generation to generation within cultures. It's not just the words, the tunes and the licks seem hard wired. We seem to have a collective knowing of folk music. Playing folk music makes me feel closer to my ancestors and those who used to live in this place.

And jazz...the structure and the freedom. Getting lost in that moment of improvisation. The simultaneous simplicity and complexity. Working hard to learn the scales, chord sequences, licks and then needing to forget it all in the moment, to get in the flow. Playing the music, but rarely playing the notes. Connecting with fellow musicians and feeding off the audience. It's exhilarating. So many metaphors in jazz.

And trance. How does music do that? Be it the rhythm of shamanic rattles and drums, or drum and base at a festival, an Arabic lament, or the music for 5-rhythms dancing. I am shifted to another place, another consciousness. It creates an opening up and deepening of my experience of myself, the world around me and connection with others. It's something about the beat, the pulse that slows my brainwaves into an alpha state. Sometimes I need to dance and dance and dance. Other times I am taken into a trance like state where I lose myself and return having experienced and learned something psychic.

These repeated experiences are part of my Becoming.

Wisdom

"I'm not trying to be wise, that would be foolish." Mary Oliver

I'm slightly allergic to the idea of trying to be wise. Not full-on anaphylaxis, but discussions about striving to be wise bring me out in a rash! About 14 years ago, I recall making a trip up to Cumbria to see my in-laws. A 6-hour journey with our kids in the back of the car. My husband and I were having an argument about something. My 7-year-old son pipes up from the back seat with a simple question 'Why are you arguing?' when I told him, his response was 'But why? That doesn't matter.' He was right and I cried. Sometimes naivety just cuts through.

The more I know, the more I realise there is so much I don't know. I reckon I know a maximum of 0.000000001% of everything there is to know…and that's probably an over-estimate and doesn't include everything we feel and everything we do. I am no expert at anything, I haven't become masterful at anything. My brain feels like a bookcase…it's got finite capacity and if I add more books at one end of the shelf, books fall off the other end, but this is all still just about knowledge and that's not the same as wisdom.

The more I realise my own failings and limitations as a human being, the more foolish I feel. The more I feel like I'm regaining naivety. Some people scorn naivety, but I reckon it's closely aligned to wisdom.

"The Fool in King Lear was the only person in the King's Court that could speak Truth to Power on account of his status as a jester."

There is something about being knowingly naïve and foolish that is wise. As I get older my own agendas seem less important. I can acknowledge that my values are a big jumble of contextually dependent contradictions, and most of the time they don't really matter.

I'm very content displaying my own naivety and growing steadily and deliberately more foolish. I can ask those naïve and wise questions like my 7-year-old son. I quite like to have a go at things and be happy getting things wrong or making a fool out of myself. It's fun to be able to say, 'I don't know' and 'Can you help me' and 'I don't understand.' I love learning from my children and I'm happy they know more than me on some subjects. I'd like to creep into my daughter's history 'A' level class and sit at the back of the class and learn all about interesting history stuff that I know nothing about.

Death and Living
"I shut my eyes, and the world drops dead; I lift my eyes and all is born again." Sylvia Plath

I have worked for 28 years in the accident and emergency department. I have seen many deaths over this time. Death is very familiar to me. Death is normal and ordinary. A part of the circle of life, except when it involves children, that feels different. There are a few cases where the faces of the child or the young mother are seared into my brain. Where when I recall the conversations with grieving shocked families' feelings of pain resurface. These are memories, where now, as I recall them, I feel powerless, small and physically sick. These are the feelings where I am not a doctor, I am a human being, a fellow parent. As I think of these people I feel like a lost soul. I want to love and just 'Be' with those families. I need to be loved too.

My husband had a near death experience. He was just 18 and had serious malaria and pneumonia. He recalls a tunnel and a bright light. A similar experience described by others who have been close to death. A fascinating shared experience and I wonder what this could mean.

My Shamanic teacher took a group of us to look at our deaths. We were taken back in time to a roundhouse. We found our way to a river together and crossed the river on stepping stones. I travelled in bare feet and the stones felt warm and smooth. As we crossed over the central balancing point in the river we meditated on the next three stones, contemplating joyful curiosity, gratitude and compassion for self and others. We travelled down the river to the sea. It was dark and the full

moon reflected in the water. I looked at my death. I sat on a
rock and looked at a beautiful calm sea, full of life. There were
no other human beings with me, but I was not alone. I felt
drawn to go in, just to see what it was like. I went for a swim in
my death, and then I returned to the rock. When I came back,
I became a big brown bird of prey. I had strong wings and
sharp eyes. I flew up the river, looking at my life's journey until
I found my birth. I perched in a tree and looked at the source
of the river as it bubbled up from amongst the roots of the tree.
I felt calm. I felt ready to live life in the moment, be present
and enjoy now and be ready for death in the next moment.

Reality
**"Underneath the reality in which we live and have our
being, another and altogether different reality lies
concealed." Nietzsche**
So, what if this reality is not the only reality? It seems to me
that there is a whole array of different realities inside our
minds which come to me in my dreams. Sometimes it feels
like dreams come into my mind from outside of me, maybe to
help other people. It feels like there are other realities
too…quantum physics seems to suggest there might be and
blows the idea of linear time into another dimension. Can we
access them? Does western culture domesticate us into
blocking out other realities? Are we conscious as individuals
or is there a meta-collective consciousness that we are tuned

in to, or both? Other cultures seem to be more open to the existence of other realities. Realities that could appear alongside this consensus reality. But here in the west, I would probably be diagnosed with some sort of psychosis if I admitted to experiencing more than one reality.

Then there are fractals...repeating patterns, like an ever-evolving unfolding of ourselves and the world around us. Repeating patterns all around us in flowers, the British coastline, weather patterns and in the way homo sapiens think and interact and how organisations function. My Dad was a quantum physicist and I remember him on the TV talking to Patrick Moore about fractals back in the 80's. I struggled to understand his explanation despite spending a chunk of my childhood looking at refraction patterns in the swimming pool, and sparkle patterns from the sun reflecting on the sea and hearing the coastline analogy.

I wonder what draws me to exploring this stuff? Part of me hopes it's my ancestors that are beckoning me in. Trying to introduce me to other worlds, their worlds. I want to explore this more, but not in a way where I scare myself or end up in a mental health unit! And basically, Star Trek has got this stuff nailed.

Fitting in...or not

"I don't expect people to get me. That would be quite arrogant. I think there are a lot of people out there that nobody gets." Bjork

So, I feel like I've become a shape shifter. I started by sharing my love of exploring the space where science, myth and spirituality come together, but of course sometimes I exist in each one of those spaces independently. I couldn't do my Shamanic stuff while working in the hospital, my hospital colleagues would think I had gone mad. Equally I wouldn't offer a course of tranquillisers to an anxious coaching client. Maybe this is where the 7th alchemical process comes in. 'Coagulation' the final transformation. A coming together of all the different parts. I have been there more than once, but not right now. Right now, I feel like I'm at the 6th alchemical process. A phase of distillation, repeated separation, and combination of multiple selves until a new form arises. These multiple selves are all constructed anyway and open to deconstruction as and when the time is right and then reconstructed in another format if needed. And, of course, the alchemical process never stops, it just keeps on going round and round, burning, distilling, coagulating, burning again, distilling and coagulating. Part of me thinks that's what coaching could be about.

And then there's coaching

Ah yes...I have been on the receiving end of coaching, and that unblocked some internal no entry signs and kick started me on this journey. I have done an accredited coaching qualification, and it was interesting, and I did learn stuff, some of which I've used and some of which I've put in my back pocket and some of which I've pushed to the back of my bottom drawer. It gave me a badge, a credibility in the eyes of others, namely clients' and my organisations. Was it the making of me as a coach? In short…no. My own 'Becoming' has been infinitely more important.

Being Weird
"She walked quickly through the darkness with the frank stride of someone who was at least certain that the forest, on this damp and windy night, contained strange and terrible things and she was it." Terry Pratchett, Wyrd Sisters
I guess that brings me back to the first quote. Now that I understand the derivation of the word weird, I'm rather attracted to it. The idea of evoking the sense of 'Unearthly' seems quite apt. Have the 'Power to control destiny' is appealing if a little over the top, but I'll settle for that.

Meta-Becoming
"When you consider things like stars, our affairs don't seem to matter too much, do they?" Virginia Woolf
Science, mythology and spirituality coalesce. I live in a scientific age and I embrace this along with my deeply human

need for spirituality. A need that lay buried inside me, but was gestating ready to wake, birth and grow when the conditions were right. A need that has also allowed me to explore and embrace my shadow side and knowingly hold my dark and light sides together in paradox. One defines the other, one can't exist without the other. Whilst embracing this part of myself and recognising the reality of who I am, this knowing can leave me feeling alone. And, this paradox of light and dark is everywhere, it's how we human beings live, but most of the time we are blind to it. There are times when I dare to pull up the blinds and confront the darkness, but I can only bear it for a microsecond. Then I have to pull the blinds back down, because I am not ready yet. There are other times when I find myself feeling connection and compassion for all living things. I lie on this beautiful green and blue jewel in space, and gaze at the stars blinking at me from the past, wondering what is in store for my children and future generations. I don't know where I end and the universe begins, somehow, we merge. I am here for just a flicker in time, and I feel at once powerful and irrelevant.

Conclusion

So in conclusion…there is no conclusion. Becoming just keeps becoming. It ebbs and flows, shrinks and expands. It unravels, ravels, and unravels again. Eventually we die and then we become compost in the earth and hopefully we become the fertile soil for a new life, a new becoming. Maybe our soul keeps on becoming in another way, in another place.

The Becoming… Bob Garvey

It all started way back in the late 1970s. I was a primary school teacher. I hadn't been teaching very long when an advisory teacher came to see me. He suggested I did a primary science course for two weeks. They would cover my teaching with a supply teacher. My Headteacher, Roy, agreed. This was the beginning. The whole course was about questions and fair tests. It was also great fun! I was hooked on to a non-directive, enquiry-based approach to primary education.

I moved with my wife Margaret and our baby daughter Frances to West Sussex to take up the post of Deputy Head of a two-form entry primary school. It was hell! In the staff's eyes, I was the whizz kid from London who had been appointed above their preferred candidate. The Headteacher told me she would back me, but I had to take the staff on and drag them out of the dark ages of education.

I was 'sent to Coventry', had doors slammed in my face and generally the focus of bad behaviour from the staff. I was different and they made me feel it. I was experiencing prejudice; unsubstantiated assumptions being made about me. It was an extraordinary experience and yet formative.

I achieved a lot there in my 2 years and 1 term! I changed the way the staff displayed the children's work. I directed many musical performances and plays - something else the staff didn't do. I started mixed cricket – unheard of because only boys played cricket! I got parents on my side by doing evening workshops on enquiry-based learning and this put pressure on the other teachers to change their ways. This made me more unpopular! I got to work early and left late. I learned from the Headteacher, what it was like to be supported. Her mantra was "don't confront anyone, there is no way back from confrontation." I didn't, but I wasn't a push over either. I learned to stand up for myself.

I wrote this story about one of the pupils. It's in my PhD thesis…

A True Story - Terry

Terry was the child of a single parent. Born into poverty. Not talked to. Left to play on the street. Brought himself up. School was no better. It was alien. He didn't fit in. All the other children could read. They talked differently. Could do sums. Could draw. Play instruments. They were good at sport. Terry wanted to be good at sport. But nobody took any notice of him. He didn't push himself forward.

But he showed them.

He could fight. He could shout and push the other kids over. They didn't fight back very often. He got into trouble with the teachers. So what? He didn't care. Why should he? What could they do to him that was worse than he had got?

Day after day. Week after week. Year after year he endured his time at school.

He dreaded Mondays because everybody would be asked to write about the weekend. He couldn't write much. Didn't want to write much. Anyway, his weekend was spent in the garage with bits of wood, making things. That was his secret.

Each teacher, each year would make him spend all of Monday writing nothing.

All the other kids (except Tony, who was just like him) finished in no time. By playtime they were doing other things.

Not Terry.

He would wait in the 'words' queue for ages. Each time he got close to the teacher he would move himself to the back of the queue. This put in the time after all.

Then, he might push a kid who looked at him strangely. Terry would be told off for 5 minutes.

This put in more time.

He might go to the toilet for 25 minutes. He might pee up the wall. Scratch swear words in big letters in the paint. (He could spell all the swear words. He had heard them enough times.) He might get caught or blamed. It got him some attention. It put in more time.

Sometimes, during playtime, he would have to stand outside the Head's office for doing something naughty.

This was good.

He could see everything that happened outside the Head's door. All the to-ings and fro-ings of the teachers. He could hear what they said in the staff room too. And some teachers would come up to him and say "Oh Terry, are you in trouble again? What are we going to do with you?"

Terry would hang his head and look forlorn. Distressed.

He wasn't. He didn't care.

It put in the time.

Some teachers would come and yell at him. "Terry, I'm sick and tired of seeing you outside here, you are nothing but a nuisance. What are you?"

Terry would dutifully mumble "A nuisance sir/miss".

One teacher might then say "Don't mumble lad, I asked you a question. What are you, eh?" "Yes, that's right a nuisance."

Tuesdays were the same as Mondays. Except, Tuesdays started with Maths. Book 1 or 2 or 3 depending on which year you were in.

It made no difference to Terry. He couldn't do it anyway.

This was the pattern of things. Day after day. Week after week. Year after year.

A positive educational experience?

Friday afternoon was different. Everyone got to go onto the field to play games.

Terry rarely did.

He was usually in trouble.

His punishment was always to tidy the classroom. (They couldn't even think of a better 'punishment'.) He was left alone.

He loved it.

He could tidy the room. He did it well.

When he had finished, he would look at the fish in the library. He might pull out a book. He would always look at the picture of the Dreadnought class battleship. He loved that picture. He knew every inch of it. He could even read some of the words. He didn't tell. That was his 'power'. He could draw it from memory.

When the end of Friday finally came, he would run home. Pushing all the other kids out of his way. In a hurry to get to his garage. He was building his Dreadnought battleship. A perfect scale model. It was his secret. He would make each little bit with great care and precision. It was his.

Terry grew older. The gulf between him and the other children deepened. Eventually he reached the final year. He was to have a new teacher. The new teacher was Deputy Head. The last Deputy Head used to give him a whack now and again when some of the other teachers had had enough of him.

Terry didn't know what to expect from this new teacher. Terry went into class. He kept his head down. He rarely looked up. He might get noticed if he did.

Then the day came.

He was called up to read.

He couldn't. The new teacher didn't seem to mind.

The new teacher was quite nice to him. He talked to him, asked him questions and found out what he liked, and Terry found himself telling him his secret. He didn't know why he did, and he didn't regret it because the new teacher said that if he liked making models, he could. And, he could do it in lesson time.

The class were 'doing' the first world war as their project. Terry had his big chance; he could make a Dreadnought Battleship. This new teacher had loads of balsa wood and all the tools. This was much better than the scraps of wood he could get together in his garage.

The teacher talked to Terry about his model, asked him about size and proportion, they talked about scale and looked at pictures of the Dreadnought together. The new teacher was interested. Terry started to feel quite good about school.

He started to make his model. It would be good. It would be the best he had ever done. It would be right, and this teacher would be pleased.

The rest of the children in the class started to take an interest in what Terry was doing. They were interested in the fact that

Terry was allowed to make his model all day. That was alright because the new teacher let them do interesting things too. He didn't make them do page after page of the same type of sums. He didn't make them write about a boring weekend; he didn't make them do page after page of 'First Aid in English'. He set them problems. He let them set their own problems. He joked with them and talked to them about their work. He joined in with their projects. He took photos of them working. They took photos of their work. They made films. Wrote music. Told stories. Solved problems. Did real sums. Did computering. Found out things. Looked at things. Drew real pictures of real things. Did science. Did projects in groups. Talked to each other. Had a great time.

This teacher even invited the mums and dads to come to school in the evening to do projects and science and sums and things. The mums and dads liked it too.

Terry's model progressed well. It was the best thing he had ever done. He knew that. The teacher said it was "brilliant". The kids in the class said it was "ace".

Terry felt good. Good for the first time.

The other kids let him play cricket in the playground. They said he was good at it.

The new teacher played cricket in the playground with them too. He asked Terry to play for the school team.

This new teacher didn't hit anybody. Miss Jones sent kids to him for a whack all the time. He didn't give them one. He talked to them instead.

Terry suspected that this new teacher was unpopular with the other teachers. He didn't really understand what it was all about, but he had seen things and heard things when he stood outside the Head's office. He heard shouting from the staff room once. He had never heard that before. Once he saw Mr. Brown slam the door in the face of the new teacher and Mr. Brown didn't say sorry. He did it on purpose. Another time, the new teacher was in the middle of saying something about not hitting children to Miss Jones when she just walked away as if he didn't exist. This wasn't a mistake. Miss Jones heard. She gave Terry a 'look' as she rushed off.

Another time, Terry heard a conversation. It was a strange one. Mr Everard had a small beetle in a match box. He had shown it to Terry. Mr Everard shoved the beetle under the new teacher's nose and said "If you know about science, what's this called?"

Terry thought that this was a strange way to talk - especially to the Deputy Head. The new teacher said "Harry!" and laughed. Terry thought that was funny. Mr. Everard did not laugh. He marched straight into the staff room. Terry couldn't hear what he said. He knew it wasn't very nice by the loudness of his voice. The new teacher followed him into the staff room. It went silent when he walked in.

Then there was the time the teachers all gathered around the display boards in the entrance hall. They were whispering about bad spelling. Terry knew they were talking about his teacher. He didn't like it. The display on the board was from his class. He thought it was great. In fact, it was his poem they were pointing at.

This new teacher couldn't be mucked about. He was everywhere and always seemed to turn up around the school when something was happening. He didn't spend all his time in the staff room like the others did. He did playground duty and went out to the playground at lunch time. Kids didn't want to muck him about. He gave everyone a chance. He didn't blame the same old kids when things went wrong. He let everyone come to cricket practise, even the girls.

Terry's model was going well. The teacher suggested that he wrote something about the model. Terry didn't mind. He would try. Nobody would laugh at him. He knew that. So, he tried. The teacher helped him, and he tried. He wrote it on the computer. Nobody had let him on the computer in the past because either he never finished 'his work', or he had been naughty. The computer was for good kids in all the other classes. This teacher let him tap the keys by himself.

This class was great. Terry started to ask about reading. He started to ask about sums. He measured the Dreadnought and tried to read about it. Terry's behaviour in the playground improved. There was no need to fight anybody. There was no need to nip off to the toilets to write things on the wall. When he had finished his model, the new teacher asked him to show it to the whole school in assembly. Terry had been in front of the whole school before but never for doing anything well or right.

All the kids said "brilliant" and gave him a clap when they saw the model. The other teachers couldn't believe what was happening either.

What was happening to the well-established pattern of winners and losers, failures and successes?

How had Terry achieved something when his destiny was to be a waster?

The new teacher was fearful of the future for Terry in the next school. But, here and now Terry was a hero.

I wrote another story about my experience and relationship with my Headteacher…….

Joy and Bob

Joy was the Head of the school. This was her second post as Head. She had transformed her first school.

The new Deputy Head was young (the youngest Deputy in West Sussex at 28 years old). He had come from the Inner London Education Authority. That, by definition put him in conflict with his teaching colleagues. The young city lad coming into the country. They felt threatened by his approach and very presence.

Initially he was in conflict with parents who were anxious about the tales of what was 'going on' at school. However, he had support from Joy. She had appointed him to do a job of work. Bob ran evening workshops for parents. They did the same things that their children did during the day. They were amazed. Joy supported these workshops. None of his colleagues came.

The pupils learned in a way they had never learned before. Their parents realised this. They noticed a change in their children's behaviour. They liked this. Parents asked why other teachers were not teaching in this way?

The conflict between the new teacher and parents reduced but it increased among his teaching colleagues. They slammed doors in his face, shouted at him in the staff room. The most difficult to deal with was being sent to 'Coventry'.

Despite the constant and daily conflict with teaching colleagues his actions and words were congruent in his dealings with staff and pupils. He was "walking the talk". He developed coping mechanisms and these were mainly focused on avoiding the staff room and spending time around the school with the children. This strengthened his position with the children and their parents. It weakened his position with staff, although a couple started to show interest in what he was doing. One admitted that she had never had the courage to work like this, but in future she would.

The key coping mechanism was regular 'chats' with Joy. Despite her being his direct boss, she was also his partner in the change process. She supported and encouraged him at every step.

Teaching colleagues constantly looked for opportunities to catch Bob out. If they found one, they rushed to tell Joy. Once, Bob put children's work on the wall in the entrance hall. It was beautiful. He had displayed it beautifully. There was a spelling mistake in one of the poems. The other teachers couldn't wait to point this out to Joy. They didn't point it out to Bob. They chose the moment of most embarrassment. Joy publicly took his side. In private they talked. He didn't want to change the child's work, but Joy helped him see that he had to. Bob quietly corrected it when everyone had gone home but not in red pen!

On another occasion, the caretaker's keys had gone missing. They were later found hidden in the boys' toilets. Bob decided that it was important to identify the culprit. His approach was to 'punish' the innocent in the hope of exposing the guilty.

This meant keeping all the children in school at play-times until someone confessed or informed.

Joy suggested privately that this was an error. Publicly she supported him.

The punishment continued for an entire week, every play time. Bob got increasingly irritated and frustrated. He had made a stand and had to see it through.

By Friday he changed his approach. He offered an amnesty if someone confessed privately at any time before the end of school. He didn't want it to go on another week! During lunch time cricket, a child whispered a confession. He was the most unlikely child, but he was distraught. Bob talked to him, and it emerged that the child had confessed without being guilty. This was to restore order. Bob viewed this as a supreme piece of moral sacrifice.

He called all the children together. He told them that he had an anonymous confession and that was the end of it.

In the evening, after school he discussed it with Joy. Without criticism they discussed the isJoys and he understood where he had 'gone wrong'. Through a painful and frustrating experience, he had learned something about leadership, decisions and judgements.

Joy could have intervened at any time. She let him learn through experience and offered support, an opportunity for reflection and discussion after the experience.

Joy introduced Bob to every visitor. She invited him to every discussion with parents. She invited him to interview every new member of staff. She invited him to meetings with County officers. She sought opportunities to promote his work at every turn. She told him who was who. Who to cultivate, who to avoid and how to handle certain people. They discussed his future career. She posed problems. Delegated difficult tasks. Left him to make blunders. Encouraged him to take initiative in this school and in other schools in the County. They discussed the day to day running of the school, the pupils, the staff, the parents the education office. They discussed his family, her family and the state of the English cricket team!

In two very traumatic, tense, busy and rewarding years Bob became well known in the County. It was only a matter of time before he became a Head himself. Joy knew this. She used to say to him, "I'll give you three years. I'll make you work really hard and after three years you'll be off. But this school will benefit greatly from your influence."

After two years, Bob resigned. After two years and one term, he left to look after his new baby and reflect on his experience. This shocked Joy at first. But she knew that Bob was unorthodox. She accepted his decision.

Bob kept in touch with Joy regularly for about three years. Still discussing things of interest. He only visited the school once after leaving. She also helped him to be 'up-to-date' with educational issues. Bob went to visit her just after she retired. They got on just as well as before.

Fourteen years later, they exchanged Christmas cards.

Fifteen years later, Joy died from cancer.

So, this chapter closes and what has been learned?

Terry was in what Jarvis (1992) called a 'non-learning' state for most of his schooling. This included elements of Jarvis' (1992) 'presumption' - he had an expectation of the school experience and he simply behaved in line with his presumptions. His 'non-learning' state also included a large element of 'rejection'. The school experience was so alien to him that 'rejection' was the easiest option. It may also be possible that Jarvis' (1992) 'non-consideration' of the school experience as holding anything of value for him played a part in his 'non-learning' at school.

In Terry's case he certainly was learning his place and was most definitely being kept in it by the education process - outside of mainstream society and in a backwater of anti-social behaviour.

As the narrative suggests, his failure was being compounded and reinforced by the teachers. They had created a self-serving system which provided them with a role and a function - an identity and Bob was threatening it by his very presence. Additionally, the staff at the school provide another link to the idea of 'non-learning'. In general, they were also stuck in all three elements of 'non-learning' – 'resumption'; 'non-consideration' and 'rejection'. They wanted their world to remain as it was and were therefore operating on a series of 'presumptions'. They found the challenge of change perhaps too much to contemplate and therefore preferred 'non-consideration' and at times hostile 'rejection' of the learning offered by a change in approach to education that I had presented.

Terry did not have learning difficulties. He was not 'thick' or disruptive. He did not misbehave to spite his teachers, as they believed. He was just 'switched off' by the environment, the social context was not appropriate for his needs. So far in life, Terry had learned the things he wanted to without difficulty. He had a great capacity to learn. His potential was not exploited. It was simply suppressed by a context which was inappropriate for him. The environment I created at the school was one based on relationships. I was supportive, respectful, challenging, honest, trusting. I encouraged laughter, risk taking, investigation, experimentation, participation.

I did not plan 'lessons' for I did not view learning as a series of lessons lasting 35 minutes. This is not to say that I did not know what I was doing or that I was engaging in random chaos. I saw learning as an holistic, continuous process which should be pursued until the issues were resolved. In Jarvis's (1992) terms, with full consideration of experiential learning. In Vygotskian terms as a 'unity of perception, speech and action, which ultimately produces internalization' (Vygotsky, 1978, p.26) If, for Terry, this took 35 minutes that was alright. If it took a day, a week, a month, that was also alright. All this was pre-National Curriculum. A member of Her Majesty's Scholl Inspectorate visited my classroom. He stood in the doorway and saw activity of various types. I invited him to talk to the children. He asked to see my records of the children's progress, which I provided. His comment was "For the first time in my career, I see real education going on here!"

I was leaving it, I saw what was on the horizon with the National Curriculum.

Our second child was born on the day of my leaving 'do'. I couldn't attend! Thank you, Katherine!

I then spent two years being a full-time Dad. I learned more about prejudice or was it fear or suspicion as I was rejected from 'Mother and baby groups' for being a man!? My opinions on looking after babies was ridiculed. For example, I was challenged on why I had my daughter in the harness facing outwards rather than the conventional inwards! I said it was because she needs to see the world and not my chest! I was laughed at when I suggested that babies needed 'white noise' to sleep – I used to put on the vacuum cleaner – it worked! These things are common now

.

In the evenings I wrote teachers' notes for BBC Schools Radio.

We left West Sussex, where they don't bother to count the Tory vote, they just weigh it, and moved to York! A friend introduced me to a management development consultant in York. I joined the MaST Organisation as a senior educational consultant. Despite MaST being full of Tories, it also had strong views on facilitation of learning. My boss used to run a 3-day management development programme with nothing but a list of questions.

One of my clients was Durham University Business School. The school engaged me to deliver a management development programme for consultant doctors – the first of its type in the UK. There were many cohorts of doctors, and I was at Durham regularly. These were basically experiential learning courses based on activities, questioning, listening, challenge and support. Building relationships was crucial to this way of working. Eventually, I started delivering courses for Durham staff on facilitating learning and presentation skills and this led to me being asked to create a job for myself at Durham.

So, I became an academic and I suffered with imposter syndrome – BIG TIME! I somehow got through that in time. The regional NHS boss came to see me one day. He had heard that I was doing a PhD on mentoring and he wanted me to design a mentoring programme for the NHS. So, I did! During this time, I received a letter (remember those!) from David Clutterbuck. He and David Megginson had created an organisation called the European Mentoring Centre and they were inviting me to join their first conference in Sheffield. I joined an I went. There were a small number of people there and all were interested in mentoring. I became involved.

Time moved on. An opportunity to move to Sheffield Business School appeared. I started work with David Megginson and Paul Stokes and we established the Coaching and Mentoring Research Unit. We were on the crest of a wave with so much interesting work and a newly created master's programme which we devised and took to Switzerland as well as facilitating it in the UK.

A pause now for some reflections.

So, learning matters! The context or environment in which it happens matters and makes a difference. Learning is about questions, listening and supportive challenge. Learning happens in relationships. Some people make assumptions and project their assumptions onto others. These can be prejudicial. Some people really don't like change or anything that is not with their mental frame. Through relationships and learning, things can change.

In our research 'On becoming a coach: Narratives of Learning and development', a common experience was a 'life's event'. These took many forms but all contributed to how the coach had become.

For me, there have been some of these. One is characterised by 'loss'.

My mother died from cancer when I was 19. This was a great loss for me at a formative period of my life. She taught me how to cook, sew and various other domestic tasks. She said, "No son of mine is leaving home without knowing how to look after himself !" My mother was a woman of great strength. She had strong values. She was a Christian and did a lot of work to support other people. She was very creative, she could paint and do the most amazing embroidery. She got commissions to make Church vestments. These were amazing pieces of embroidery with deep symbolic images and bright colours on them.

I think I admired her creativity, her boldness and her values and her practical nature. Some has rubbed off on me maybe? I had a girlfriend at that time and we later married. Here is the second loss. After two years of marriage, one day she said that she didn't love me anymore and moved out. This was a shock and a loss. I didn't see it coming, a blindness. It took a few years to gain a new sense of direction. I met Margaret and we were together for forty years.

The next loss was, Joy, my Headteacher and mentor. A time for reflection….

Years moved on and my big sister was seriously ill. We had a telepathic relationship. It was strange. She died, terrified that God would punish her sins. I lost faith many years before and this ridiculousness, this pain this sense of guilt that my sister felt was a result of her faith. Some years before, she had sign-up to the born-again movement and this is what it gave her back.

The next lost was my father. He became, after a few years where I couldn't relate to him (this was after my mother died), he became my very best friend. He moved into the house next door to me for 8 years and I spent time with him. He was an intelligent man with many artistic gifts, his wit being one of them! He always had a twinkle in his eye and was there with a quip or a joke. I related to his calmness, almost serenity in his later years. He was 97 when he died and his only regret was not being 100!

The next loss was Margaret.

I always thought we would grow disgracefully old together

I always thought we would grow disgracefully old together
You with your porcelain skin

And your figurine posture

Your acerbic wit

And the voice of an angel

I always thought we would.

But, the cancer grew in your brain

Crab-like

You built a crustacean's shell

You shut down in lockdown

Impenetrable and into silence you went

And, one day in springtime

You fell into an eternity of silence

I always thought we'd grow disgracefully old together ......But,

I was wrong.

On the other hand, loss builds something. My positive outlook never diminishes. Is that resilience? How can one go on a resilience course to learn resilience without experience to draw upon? That doesn't make sense to me!

Then there is a period of calm. The loss is always with me. The pain changes but it never goes away and sometimes it jumps out behind a bush and gets you! Is that what enables compassion and thoughtfulness for others? Empathy, understanding.

Another 'life event' was the experience of serious illness. I was unwell for 12 years and I finally had major abdominal surgery, twice! Each procedure lasted over 8 hours and left me very weak for nearly a year. I learned to be calm and patient. My father was that as well, maybe I caught that off him or maybe my illness contributed.

So, I am here, with characteristics that have taken many years to evolve. Attitudes, values and behaviours that have grown and changed over time. I still am not a push over and stand up for myself but perhaps with more humility than previously.

And so, we come to coaching. I don't like that word! I relate, listen and enquiry. I empathise, challenge and support. I bring myself to the discussion as best I can.

Memo – Olwyn Mary Hughes

My DNA has existed for ever in the human genome, yet I am pure accident. I am not alone, I am many faceted, but only one side is me. I am connected, communicating with a web of other lives as trees are connected by a web of mycelia. Webs connect indirectly and are never still, never silent, for the present is highly unstable. Sometimes this experience is violent, knocking me off course, sometimes it is a barely felt, subliminal stroke. In turn, I can touch - damage even - any number of others; it takes more than one to tango a crash or a stroke, after all.

So, given a choice, my place is in the unregulated, unknowing borderlands that cross in the web where lives overlap; nomad lands where are ricochets, accidents, stickiness and general messes and in which nothing is native. Here, many stories and transports emerge and evolve into other beings and doings: there needs to be a primordial soup to cause and nourish evolution, after all.

Some worry about messes, but I notice they are not of concern rather it is the purity of intention and attention given to the formation of evolving that matters. This lighting-up may be what torch-lit the coach in me but also may be hot enough to torch it.   Whether any of it ever became or un-became me - made me a coach - is, likely, for the reader to work out for themselves.

So, here are some stories for the reader to judge.   It is no autobiography. Myths appear and so do snapshots, also histories, parables and wandering tales, the stories that turn on themselves because they have no end. None of what follows is linear as the web cannot die, is never a flatline. It is just my ever-shifting viewpoint which means I should caution the reader because, whether they will or not, they have now crossed with me and are connected, as am I with them. A cost (or reward) of judging.

Once whilst waiting in a cold corridor for another person, I began to get acquainted with my irritability because this felt a more useful way to pass time than fulminating. The relationship explained itself as entrapment, time spilling forward while I was involuntarily immobile except, I noticed, I was far from stationary. I was going backwards. I was all over the past - my past - wading in remembering and it all feeling strangely unfamiliar, needing to be explored, interpreted maybe. It occurred that, for most of humanity, my past cannot have happened at all and that worked the other way round too, others' pasts never happened for me. So, what was I playing with? If I have no memory of something it never happened, at least I am wholly unknowing of it unless it is given to me, in which case, it has to be established in my memory by proxy, by someone or something. But this entails using a language, including tactile, olfactory, visual and audio languages to switch on understanding, trust and belief about what I am being given. I understand the past and memory as wholly different things, the past cannot be retrieved because it is spent, but memory is volatile, timeless and the only substance with which to shape, explain and show what has happened and imply what might happen.

Deities are useful for simplification. So, I have Mnemosyne (pronounced 'Mneem-o-seen-ee') in mind.   She is a Titan, the ancient Greek goddess of memory and language and the daughter of heaven and earth, of Uranus and Gaea. The altar of her worship is the notion that our lives are not the past, but the substance of heaven and earth conjoined, creating memory which is abstract, elemental and so strongly formative. Later Greeks struggled with her abstractness and, pairing her off with that most lascivious of all gods-of-testosterone, Zeus, had her parent the nine Muses so they could categorise her effect. Mnemosyne is a most helpful supernatural phenomenon, for starters she tells me that my reflective loitering in a corridor had weight.   Moreover, a weight pulled on by Olympic-grade Greek philosophers.

Myths are the memory of a people. Scholars may call this a 'collective unconscious' however I see a DNA-like collection of words passed on over millennia as a contract between teller and listener. The jobs are different, one gives and the other receives while between them shimmers a refractive, reflective, reflexive atmosphere. Within this atmosphere, all manner of beings can breathe and grow, some becoming sufficiently relatable to lodge in the web and be shared. Many are simply forgotten by people, much as ancestry is forgotten (there is simply too much of it). But the web won't let them go, which is different from being forgotten, they become DNA and everyone's ancestry: at some point they emerge again as mythic memory.

Hanes Taliesin ('Hanes' means history or story in Cymraeg, Welsh) has always re-cited itself when I face the past. First told to me by a great-aunt then by a book with the same status as my teddy bear, *Welsh Folk Tales,* (it contained many of the *Mabinogi,* stories I invite the reader to find, if they have not already) I have always held the listener's contract. Let me now be the teller:

So Gwion Bach became a grain of corn and Ceridwen a black hen and she ate him. The shapeshifting hunt started when he tasted the splash of enchantment, magic and divination from her cauldron and now ended with her win. But, no: nine months later she gave birth to Taliesin, the Shining One of bards - her child brought up by adoptive parents who adored him: Gwion won. But, no: follow the web: Perhaps art and poetry are incubated and born of enchantment, magic and divination and must be loved, as was Taliesin, to exist and survive.

Without Ceridwen, however, the tale has no reason or shape to shift anywhere. She started it all and Taliesin is a result, a consequence although he is these days celebrated while she seen as his witchy, monster mother, her hubris downed by comeuppance. This is selectivity at work to spare wincing as mores vacillate. Ceridwen's especial powers are, as in her cauldron, enchantment, divination and magic so she can make and change anything whilst being able to understand what that might foretell. She is the stuff of mythic memory, a goddess to match Mnemosyne in command of an elemental formation. In itself, memory is an inert, abstract substance, but the intention, will and energy to conjure with it invites Ceridwen's skills. I notice how memories are activated, enchanted, made magic thus allowing suggestions about what might happen next, divining the way forward often untested, yet taken in trust. Ceridwen reminds me that much can be confected from the abstract and presented selectively. In the unregulated borderlands where misrule invites memory to fandango joyfully into magical answers, intention asks quietly about enchantments and divination. Ceridwen also suggests the Muses might be unnecessary reductivism.

I lack competitiveness. I contend this is not laziness or cowardice but trying to survive, looking for clues in the territory so that I can find the handholds and the things that will take my hand and lead me into safety. My Father, propelled by a sense of being undervalued, moved us between continents searching for fulfilment, justified by duty to support my mother and my brother's development. In the slipstream, I was never in the right system, in the right place, at the right time so I missed exams and could not use an entry into university. I ended up with Canadian Grade 13 (it involved no examinations as known to UK systems) as my sole academic badge. My Mother, faced with a bemused teen, decided to enrol me into art school, her influence free because my Father's was exhausted (and I drew pictures a lot). My student grant was tiny, so I got acquainted with wages: bars, hospitals, houses, farms and shops paid for paint and rent in-between lectures and studios. Any early attempts to ask my Parents for financial help were quickly, gently stopped, they had too much else to afford. There was no time or space for limiting and exhausting competition to become much, I had to get by and get on and not waste time looking over my shoulders at who might be coming up to beat me - and what they might be wanting to beat me at (or with). I evolved needing to pay attention to the chances offered by relationships colliding, collapsing and contorting but avoid being drawn to wager or spend any of the gains. Never a game of chance, it was the magic of chance to be respected not the skill of chance to be had. All in the cause of survival and all accrued in the web.

Art school required demonstrating innate ability, academic and applied. This entailed seeming thus for the beholder, so becoming beholden. This is a becoming and an unbecoming, also a teller and a listener in visual translation. The one who gives and the one who receives and adding the question about where the kinetics for those energies are sourced and why they are wanted at all. I enacted this in several scenarios, the ethical and the fantastical together so that bulimic gorging on knowledge could be spewed out as *my* knowledge over the doorsteps of those demanding I do so, yet cover my caching of treasures to think about, long and hard. This was most tested, not just in making paintings and studying theory, but in the Crit. A Crit is when fellow students and lecturers gather to criticise you and your work out loud. You are under scrutiny and pushed to that place that brings about defence, preferably attired as knowledge. The premise is democratic critical analysis, but the reality is challenge, not infrequently coloured with shades of ridicule and competitiveness. Raw, rapid stuff of agendas framed by cultural bias, preferences, and playing the game. Thus, I learned *Taste* and how that is the only flavour in the place, a prescribed palate and never a daughter of Mnemosyne's although artists have muses. Often these are simply naked women subtitled as goddesses (more often nymphs). But I also noticed how this meant the art world repeatedly ate itself, hungry for value but somehow sure other worlds would find it indigestible and sometimes this was (and is) the case. However, tastes change and, eventually, the world inures itself into appreciating a Monet or an Emin, forgetting a Reynolds or an Morrisot. But that is beholding packaged for Taste, beholden still to images that entertain us as tastefully creative however indigestible the provenance. Some art is revered as evidence of a priceless creativity and as such is held, locked up in buildings and bank accounts. It is given value through exclusivity and the perpetration of exclusive talent. But creativity isn't about exclusion, and it may not be about talent, it doesn't really exist at all as a Thing other than it is essential to evolutionary survival because it is about ignoring the proscribed and the prescribed, finding fresh ways to reassemble and disassemble meaningfully. Call it imagination if you like though, as archaeology is a meditation for meaning on human remains, imagination is a meditation for meaning on all and any remains. I mostly did creativity because to make things from flotsam and jetsam was to escape competition and being beholden. It was also cheaper and, besides, competition's greatest achievement is loss because it forces meditation on remains and that is never failure. It can be enormous fun.

Then I taught art at secondary school for a while. This electrocuted me into somewhere between cynicism and the messianic, a frazzled entity. Teaching art meant being tasteful all over again, colluding with a preference for clever decoration over communication and dumb prettiness over expression; it depressed me. So, I fell back on how I knew to survive, on the need to make a living yet keep my faith. I suspect this was when I began to realise, I might have a philosophy and little faith. Anyway, I became a Home Civil Servant. This, then, was my career, that mad dash after cash that allowed me to submit to a place in the system my upbringing had avoided. It lasted well over thirty years. Here was I, an organ of the body corporate in that great staff of folk where collaboration and collusion are constants, doing things for an ever-revising mission calling itself, Delivery. The Civil Service mostly does this in a benign way, however, and it allowed me to stretch my socialist preference as a Trade Union representative but all, the Unions included, kept watch for the contrary wise non- collaborators.

At a point where the Department I worked for was saving money by shedding staff, I was put on an accelerated development programme, designed to get me 'on and up'. This came about because I began to be trusted as a writer and communicator of reports and analyses and because of a couple of shifts in central policy branches. It was, however, also to make me more attractive to other Departments. So, I was lent to the then Welsh Office to establish a nursery for the children of local public servants. This I did and, as a result, was accepted for a transfer. Job done. Indeed, all went well for me (and both Civil Service Departments) until my credentials were examined by a very senior officer at which point, I was summoned, exclusively, for an extra interview alone with him. The issue was that he had read my CV and was horrified to learn that the Welsh Office had transferred in someone without A Levels or O Levels and a Degree in Fine Art to an Executive posting. To his credit, the Union work was not mentioned.

The interview was a homily and a caution. My new employer had goals to accept only the highest quality staff from other Departments, people with Degrees from Universities of repute and scholastically high achievers. "You are none of these", he confirmed. My new employer also had goals for numbers of new staff with recognised records of achievement. "How, exactly, did you do that research, write those reports, create those business cases, manage those budgets and those projects?" He asked. My response about process and careful consideration, accessing The Literature etc. etc. still troubled him to the extent that I was asked what my husband did and whether I had worked with people whose qualifications outstripped mine. My answers appeared to increase his distress and thus began a sort of probation year which my work was subject to moderating scrutiny and reported on.

It was not recommended I be put into critical policy work, but HR where I could (I have always surmised) be watched. Union colleagues advised me to make an official complaint about this interview, but I never did as it seemed so inconsequential and more akin to a raised eyebrow than a body blow. In the end, nothing much more occurred and I seemed to find a place in the general jigsaw of the organisation. The body corporate is always as naked as the Emperor of China and as addicted as he to enchantment and magical thinking. The body corporate is, as well, a borderland, full of accidentally accrued fragments upon which to meditate and from which to divine the surest survival. The body corporate, however, likes neither portrait.

Decades later and after three promotions, I took early severance, it being my decision and a firm sidestep not a jump. I had outlasted many colleagues, made some truly good friends and my web connections had been vastly increased, widened with so many things to store in memory. One of these things was coaching, another was an idea about the importance of borderlands.

I am five years old and Paddington Station bustles with travellers, criminals, lovers and businesses, the air is chewy as stale rice and tastes of headaches. The Relatives put us in springy cars smelling of hot leather, cigarettes and petrol, motion and regular sick all at once. Wedged between Parents, each topped by a smaller sibling, I feel London passing by without coherence. A sleepy sister flops over, Mother's arm catches her fall, and it clears the window for me to look through. The girl stands at the top of some doorsteps in a strobe frame of vertical white pillars and horizontal black railings, described by slashed, pink sunshine, watery, purple shadows and a ransom of jewel hues in blues and golds. I am thrilled with the beauty of it. Then gone; the moment created from the accidental mess of the moment.

Beauty, abstract sense-making, moves profoundly, as do all revelations. Those clichéd, socially mediated aphorisms found on the t-shirts and personal profiles of so many who coach about finding beauty are, as I understand, really a statement about what isn't beautiful, defining what their taste is. Embarrassment harnessing sentimentalised memes to defend something potentially excruciatingly unsophisticated. Beauty is not beholden to anything or anyone; it is not in the eye of the beholder; it is free to be chosen. This is a source of so much pain that beauty is repeatedly muffled as taste, as transient yet insistent fashion. Today, I looked through windows in hope of transporting, lovely images, tomorrow I shall do the same because that is how I am allowed to understand what art is.

I need to be reminded about what is beautiful and so its place in my mind does not dim, although I may avoid it sometimes. I grew up in the Far East and among so many Faiths that I learned to conflate beauty with behaving by the preferred Book. Beauty was conformation so the makeup of choice always ensured no surprises, particularly for women. You can tell a Faith by its women (sometimes its men too, to be fair) and by its dislike of being surprised, for which reprisals can be harsh, and which sees predictability as a virtue. Here, my goddesses are pagan and their notion that it is the conjunction of memories that accesses the mysterious is banished and replaced with a singular, dictated mono-litany called Truth, where the mysterious is out of reach. Me-the-child was desolate about this and the way it informed me that I could not be rewarded by beauty emerging from the chaos I saw all about me, instead I should wait for it to be bestowed as an embellishment, should I ever attain sufficient virtue.

But I saw the sadhus with overflowing bellies, wilting frangipani and siva-ash smeared faces assumed transcendence and thus ignored the monsoon. In their cave, were macaques mating, masturbating, defecating and fighting, passing time as the storm passed in a place of diamonded ferns glittering around the cave's entrance in short bursts of sun. Stone Ganesh was grubby and the Faithful gave him decaying things, firm that they were not of the naughty tribe of Hanuman. In the Masjid a man prayed towards Mecca, quietly, gracefully prostrating himself under the gold painted ceiling and surrounded by shining tiles. He asked for peace and abundance, grace and acknowledgement of his submission to virtue while, in the street, his daughter recited, "Look up at the sky and your Mother will die".

Outside, beyond the boundary of carefully tended grounds, the crystal sand, sketched through with grasses inland and ablaze with reflection seawards, glowed its contrast with the great, green ocean. On that shore, with nothing virtual about it, birds submitted to the now tranquil day accepting peace as the wages of unruly weather and found abundant food to fuel them for the next gales in the path of the last ones. In a nearby Church, the rituals were said, and the old building looked on, from a ghostly past of critical observers monkeying around as gorgeous gargoyles, marvellous misericords, superb sheela-na-gigs and glorious green men. Given weighty tablets of stone, the Faithful struggled wearily through the inconvenience of rainbows in Spring rain as it gave life to a graveyard.

Attention to The Place matters more than The Job. Stones warm and cool with the atmosphere and so do I, within and without. This is the Yin and Yang, the balance of death and life of nourishment and survival the impossibility of dark without light. Being human, I seek understanding through language, so I read a lot, accessing the recorded syllables of authors' memories, without a plan but with compulsion to find meaning. When Mother and Dad died within days of each other, words were made and gave me the comforting company of humans, but courageous comfort came from where animals, vegetables and minerals explained that all was well and all would be well because they cared without power. The bloody remains beneath a peregrine's butchering perch or the gnawed heather on the moor are testament to all life's existential relating, a parasitic relationship I am part off and to deny that is to deny how deeply I love it. I learn from science about life but understand love as the piece missing in philosophies because it drives curiosity and that lifts the blindness of fear. Curiosity may be the silk of the web, the organically produced substance that propels strong interconnectivity. Love may be the stability of the web; it produces curiosity and fear in equal measure.

I am in love with much and my heart breaks often as a result, though this just makes more fragments upon which to meditate, even of something apparently irreparably broken, and make something fresh. Creativity makes not repairs. Each time, it reminds me that love and tragedy are twins existing without songs and legends of sex or sentiment but lessons of survival in the web. I once read that true love's denouement is the inability to exist, one without the other. There are many stories about this, Romeo and Juliet and Achilles' obsessive attempts to follow Patroclus to the Styx being just two examples. Novalis put it as Romantics will, 'Love is the final end of the world's history, the Amen of the Universe'. I prefer to consider love slaps us awake to the Universe, so we (and the Universe) survive maybe it's the same thing.

Love certainly wakes me up and lights up those elements of my life that matter the most, that I remember with acuity. In thinking with memory, I have no choice but to love the uncountable connections for their help in a philosophy that can make sense and can offer comfort - excitement, even - out of the unlikeliness of my life. In the unexperienced writhes the future where survival needs to be divined. In the experienced struggles the past where the elements for survival collect in the web. But both are so enormously made of the unknown that enchantment, magic and divination seem utterly necessary to try to identify and manage them and, not least among coaches, kilocalories of effort go into such arcane arts.

Nevertheless, none of this is feasible, possible or purposeful, even if it is the work of geniuses and gods, without effortlessly travelling memory which amasses as each second ticks itself off from now into the past and swallows the future. Memory, amoral and plastic, nourishes rationality, learning, meaning, sense, a reason to continue and the nudge to evolve and survive. It also feeds the darker opposites and I listen as the greatest stories fulfil their contract, telling me this is how it always has been. While it has colours I can never see, notes I can never hear, scents I cannot smell, I am part of a web of many dimensions, spaces and times in which connections are made.

All I have ever done is try to understand all this, find how to use it well and ask of it what I can become. It may be very taxing yet very simple.

I am Becoming Memory.

Smudges – Daniel Doherty

I am an accidental coach.

Learning to write, Carlisle, 1957.

'Your brain is faster than your hand.' That was the persistent refrain heard by the young boy, both in school and when among family. This remark was invariably prompted by the sight of the smudging caused by his dragging of the outside of his left-hand, his writing hand, across the once pristine page, with much mess spilling from the black inkwell via the blunt steel nib onto the page. This daily snail trail resisted all attempts to try new finger holds, while his fellow right-handed pupils allowed their prose to glide flawlessly left to right, left to right, line after line, perfectly, in the manner the nib was fashioned so to do, immaculately conceived. The coarse nib in the boy's hand, running against the grain, would tear holes in the rough paper, ink bleeding into the pages beneath, the whole jotter tainted. But his determination to get his words on the page overrode his fear of admonishment and ridicule.

No one ever said to him, 'the speed of your brain is to be marvelled at.' No one ever said, 'we understand that having to use tools designed for brains that are wired to suit a different dexterity must be awkward and frustrating for you. But solider on, you are doing your best. And you never know, more suitable pens might come along in your lifetime that allow for your innate difference.'

In the absence of such encouragement, or technological advance, he soldiered on. When set their first ever writing assignment, his composition was selected by the teacher above all of his other fellow seven-year-olds for the best-in-class award. Delighted, he stuffed his story into his scruffy leather satchel and rushed home to break the news. Mother beamed, without reading the proffered blotted pages, saying, 'I am so proud of you, son.' Father reads what is in front of him, then pronounces, 'So now we know. You will become a journalist when you grow up.' When all he really wanted to do was to keep on writing.

'Stop staring out the window and concentrate on the task in hand. Daydreaming will get you nowhere fast. Don't go blotting your copybook again,' barked the teacher. The boy's eyes shifted with reluctance from the window where the patterns of dark cloud were forming over the town to the weeping inkblots on page. He sensed in the spaces between the smudges a story pushing through.

Jesus is on the mainline.

The boy's stories are always overshadowed by the stories he is told of the life of Jesus. How could they not be, when all the stories he ever seems to be told are those of this long-haired man with the spear in his side and the thorns on his head. And all that leaking black blood dribbling through his toes towards the foot of the cross. One night he awakens from sleep with a sensation that is not so much a dream but the strongest possible premonition that Jesus is revealing himself to him. Directly to him. He feels the deepest love flowing, copiously, towards this pulsating heart that beats and seeps for him and him alone, framed by spikey shards of golden light.

One Jesus story that he keeps on returning to is that set in the temple, where Jesus overturns the tables of the money lenders. He wants to become that righteous Jesus. Another scene that enriches his daydreaming is where Jesus sits on the temple steps, with children sat at his feet, sometimes touching his hem, while they absorb the gentle lessons studded in this gentle man's every story. This boy wants to become that Jesus too. Not the one hanging above the pools of blood, splashing to the ground to blacken the earth.

His namesake uncle is a missionary priest, Father Dan, an illusory childhood presence whom the boy gets to know through this exotic relative's precipitous return to Britain, fleeing from the Mau Mau tribe in Kenya. This uncle would tell terrifying stories of machete wielding savages whose only will was to wipe out those who follow Jesus. Catholic boys are strongly pressed, from the youngest of ages, to consider entering a seminary, to become a priest, and this boy was not immune from these urgings. Did he have a calling, he kept asking Jesus, as he knelt before this mute figure hanging there on the cross. Was doubt even allowable? But then the moment came when the boy thought he might have heard God's call, a beckoning powerful enough to cause him to believe he might have been blessed with a vocation.

Later that Sunday morning, with the rituals of Mass concluded, this altar boy shrugged off his cassock in that dark vestry, his eyes on the dark shadows fall on the stone floor, while he plucked up the courage to utter to his parish priest standing there with his back to him those words that hitherto he had only muttered to himself.

'Father, excuse me, but I think... I think I have a vocation,' he stammered, barely above a whisper.
'Oh, you do, do you now? Have you told your parents?' sighed the world-weary priest, barely lifting his eyes away from putting away the sacred host and the holy wine.
'No, I have not told anyone. Father, just you, no one else.'
'Well son, you do not have a vocation,' said the priest emphatically, wiping a speck of the sacred host from his

embroidered cuff. 'Take it from me, I know about these things. I am not even sure that I had a vocation, looking back. Now go sort out the hymn books and begone with you.'

The boy jumped on his bike, downcast. When earlier that day he had visualised, himself racing home to break his jubilant news to his assembled family, now all he has was a sense of shameful retreat. He tried but failed to choke back tears, glad only that he had never told his family of his major life-decision before he fell at the first hurdle. He rarely went back to that church again, his cassock, he imagined, still idle on its peg.

Daniel's Vision Quest: Cape Town, late September 1994

I recently excavated this pretentiously named 'Vision Quest' piece, written over a weekend in my new home in Cape Town, alone and on retreat, after a summer of vast emotional upheaval and change. Its subtitle reads, 'Some important things to note about the Daniel Conundrum: what needs to be exposed and what may remain hidden.' An oddity about this heavily stained handwritten record is that, in the face of ten house moves since, during which entire archives have been discarded, this piece has resisted removal, but never read, carried from place to place, across continents, as if it were my personal Rosetta Stone. Others new of its existence, but he had never shared.

I distinctly remember authoring the piece, sat alone in my study in my house set in a high point up Table Mountain, my unimpeded gaze cast through a window framed by cascading bougainvillea to falling on the pure azure ocean lapping Robben Island. Intentionally retreating from a summer of unfolding drama on every front, I was taking time alone to figure out who I was underneath all of the doings and theatrical switches, and what discoveries I might unearth concerning my essence and my weaknesses that would assist in directing my unfolding time here, perched above the world.

As I read between the smudged lines, I find a long listing of items, including,

'I am intensely curious to explore what lies behind 'what is presented.' I know there is always more, that I want to explore. I trust my intuition. I know this is a gift.

I am keen (not always) for people to know a lot about me. I wish them to hear me say the truth.

I am capable of accurate and compassionate articulation of my own and others dilemmas and passions. I truly release passions, without quite knowing the mechanism, but it works.

I am capable of searing honesty in a relationship at the early stages. I can provoke equivalent honesty, including others self- honesty, including self-insights that might be hidden from view.

I may seem to deal well with life's external structures and processes, create pathways out of nothing, carried by passion, brilliance, capacity for challenge. But I struggle underneath.

There is a strong rescuer in me, nearer my warrior than my magician. The rescuing impulse can be easily distorted.

I am very good at brand new starts – of all types.

My freedom urge is healthy most of the time. Sometimes I feel I carry freedom for all of us, even though I am somewhat blamed, demonised at times.

In the trade-offs between freedom and security, freedom and advancement, then freedom and excitement always win. It is scary even for me.

Work is my ally and my monster, my Gollum. We are deeply co-dependent, and where there is doubt or torment that needs to be shared, or is too pitiful to be shared, we and the monster will shut others out.

Within these random line items, I discern detectable signposts that reveal where I might need to be most attentive towards the working of my shadow selves, before they overwhelm me once more. What is striking, as I read now, is that, had I read this document at regular intervals, rather than simply carry it around, hoping its wisdom might seep through to me by some osmotic process, and taken heed of its many encouragements and cautions, then my life course since might have been different.

Perhaps I should have taken it to confession.

The life of Douglas, Latvia, September 2012.

Sometimes it is useful to have your alter ego, your shadow side named for you, to give it a distinct identity. My alter ego Douglas was so named in an apartment in Latvia while on a singing adventure with a group of friends in 2012. The naming ceremony came via two Scottish women in our group who said I physically reminded them of a Douglas in their choir. At first I resisted then slowly warmed to the idea of being Douglas for them. They explained that in Scots mythology, Douglas represented a dark stream. One evening a fellow singer declared that she thought that Douglas was my Mr Hyde, who acted in counterpoint to my somewhat proper Doctor Daniel. She set me the challenge of devoting my mornings writing practice to describing Douglas and his relationship to Daniel, so they could get to know each better, and to everyone else they collide with. This is what appeared on my screen the next morning.

Douglas is an activist, a fantasist, an ironist, and a comic. He is an original plagiarist, a divine interventionist. At his best he flows but at other times he is a jerk who cannot stop interrupting. He is a confusionist, a clarifier, a gift from god, a snot nosed brat, a chameleon, a serial adapter, an experimentalist, a blabbermouth, a philosopher, a wizard and quite often a total disgrace.

Going about his work, he is a contrarian, a buffoon, a controversialist, a provocateur, a lover and a fighter. He is a Quixote, a courageous fool who cannot help but speak truth to power, but by the same token contradicts himself in so many aspects. This impulse to express himself can often get the better or the worse of him, depending on how far he takes it. He is driven by the need for freedom, fresh insight, experiment. He needs, at often inconvenient times, to quench his thirst for excitement and novel action, to impishly disrupt.

He has a compulsive need to get things down on the page. He is a writer who has been profligate and maybe squandered his gift, maybe not. He is a wanderer and searcher on the face of this world, never truly content, always restless, always thoughtful, sometimes wildly reckless in his intuitive impulses, but not always so.

He spurns control and yet at other times abandons himself to it. He is a seducer who is also quite easily seduced by all sort of people, ideas, and vainglorious projects. He can be as much charmed as he is charming, as much wishing to please as be pleased. At some basic level he is also driven by simple, obvious needs: and is often a fool for a pretty girl.

Douglas knows that I, Daniel, struggle at times to find the right place in my life for Douglas, but then even that elusiveness is part of his charm. He is an unsettling but necessary presence that pops up at times when least invited or wanted, but in other moments perfectly on time. He is irrepressible when he springs out of the psychodynamic trapdoor, when the membrane of respectability is weak. As a callow teen I devoured Herman Hess' 'Steppenwolf.' Over the years Douglas has adapted to become my own wholly idiosyncratic Steppenwolf. He can annoy and embarrass me. But even at his most gross, I feel a tender protectiveness towards him.

Throughout my working life across a variety of occupations and geographies, I have experienced the tension between the need for conventional self- presentation and monitoring of performance; and the countervailing internal pressure of Douglas's need to break out, sometimes bursting through like an alien head protruding through the institutional ribcage. I am not sure conventional me has ever really added up to much, at least not in the ritualised sense. I have never had so much as a going away party, never mind a golden watch - though I have collected five non-disclosure agreements. But then I am not legally allowed to speak of the fact they exist. Forget I wrote that.

Douglas has been the heartbeat of my best work, in all manner of ways, and others have wondered at his minor miracles, and at the allegiances he has wrought. Douglas has never worried too much about the boundaries between work relationships, friendships, family, and intimate attraction. He has, over time, muddied those boundaries too frequently and at times destructively; and at other times has built bonds that have lasted forever. At his best he is surprisingly true and honest and kind. Oh, and so I am told, amusing too.

Post conventional work settings, Douglas still seeks the buzz of disruption, of the mad rumpus. And Daniel knows that he will die inside, be hollow, without that imp being out and about in the world.

Re-attiring, Oxford, November 2017.

A necessary part of my leaving my final full-time academic post, after twelve years served in a variety of institutions, was to drive my trusty Volvo onto campus and load it up with a random collection of largely forgotten books, trophies and artefacts, including my silken doctoral gown, which I found stuffed unceremoniously on a peg behind the office door.

My next stop - post this exhumation and sealing off the scholarly tomb - was to point the car towards my next destination, a song leaders' workshop conducted in an ancient abbey. On an impulse, at breakfast the next day, I decided to make some use of my much-neglected gown before it was ultimately mothballed, with no more graduation rituals to grace, no more stifling in the summer's heat, mechanically applauding as a procession of young lives pass out before their proud parents' eyes.

I rescued my gown from the car and slipped it on, marvelling at the creases, stains and general lived-in look so characteristic of all my wardrobe, now enhanced with a whiff of stale exhaust. Sitting down for breakfast on the ancient bench beside a song leader renowned for her wit and wisdom, she asked, not unnaturally, 'what's with the gown?' I spoke of my impulse to give the gown one last airing, by way of a symbolic ending, in the setting of this ancient seat of learning.

'Ah' she reflected 'So you have just retired?' Rather shocked by the utterance of this taboo term, I blurted 'No, Not all, I do not recognise the R word.' My vehemence was uncalled for, given that her conclusion was factually accurate, and her inquiry kindly.

'Ah, I see' she countered. 'So, you are re-attiring, not retiring?' I loved that reimagining of the R word and gave her a full swirl of the reclaimed garment in recognition of her sharpness and accuracy of thought. She asked of my twelve years before the academic mast. I explained that it all began in my mid-fifties, when I was occupied with writing a narrative doctorate that was ultimately - after much struggle - to gain me the licence to inhabit the hooded gown. The doctorate was eventually titled 'On becoming an academic.' I speculated that at this turning point in my life that I may well be in the process of reversing the engines, to un-become being an academic, to shed that skin.

Slovenia 2016, leading a 'Discovering Voice' workshop.

Still feeling pumped from my leading Discovering Voice workshop at an experimental conference focussing on the aesthetics of leadership, I picked up, with no little trepidation, the pile of written feedback comments left on a table by the exit of the lecture room.

'You bring a strong free child into play.'

'You are a free spirit, a live wire, someone who demonstrates aliveness.'

'You enabled the group to sing ourselves into vibrant life.'

'Somehow, you helped us reveal and vocalise the collective song of the group.'

'You have a wild, untamed voice'.

'I thought we were going to do advanced breathing exercises, not reaching out to our ancestors through grunts and hollerings.'

'Your voice has a hypnotic quality to it.'

'You are spontaneous, have a quickness,'

'that was quite a workout the lungs. Exhilarating.'

You allow your wit to freely flow.'

'it is amazing what you see when you close your eyes and allow the sound out.'

'You do not play by the rules. You do not need to play by the rules. Let others do that.'

Library lament, London, 2017.

It is all done now.

I had been awarded my terminal degree, so said the university ordnances.

All of my development, my elopement with learning, is done.

I can put it away.

Just as I have put away for the winter

My cherished summer car

my egg yolk yellow soft top Saab.

I left her to winter in the care of a friend with a farm

On the edge of the moor.

He parked her far away from the farmstead, pressed into a thorn hedge, beside the piles of compost, near the pigs.

MY friend says he will fill my car up with chickens

who will wait for me and lay and wait and lay again until I come to collect.

But perhaps I will never collect

instead, I will simply visit now and again, to admire her patina of rust as it bleeds into the russet hedge.

But I know in my heart that I could never cash her in.

Academics talk of cashing in credit points

or even cashing in whole degrees towards other degrees.

It is a strange market, this business of cashing in learning for what – a bigger badge?

An upgrade?

How would it be if universities were to issue not credit but debit points

And award negative degrees like dark matter instead

that dark unknowing that sucks everybody and everything towards it.

At the university where I worked

there was a library that has not been replenished for nine years.

None of the knowing in there was new.

I took a certain solace in walking those empty canyons

between those cliffs of redundant knowledge that will

languish forever until some librarian silently administers a mercy killing.

The towering silence makes me want to eschew the electronic library.

Shutting down my laptop, my paptop,

I wish to return to that place of implacable print

walk the empty stacks noiselessly

taking out books I pledge never to return

I want to make them safe

I want to liberate the lib- rary

and there will of course be fines

but I am fine with fines

they are the price to pay for learning debits

for deficit learning

and I want it no more.

Navigating online deaths, Devon, 2016 – 2018.

One librarian that never made it through was a colleague of mine, Paul, a larger-than-life character whose library induction programme for new students featured deathless slides on indexing systems interspersed with photos of him in his non-work guises as Morris dancer, folk singer, hang gliderer, rap fanboy, vivid Facebook presence and general first-adopter and disruptor of the next craze to come along. He was much loved by all for his shunning of stereotypic librarian tropes. Few of us could believe that such a life force could be taken from us on a cruel biological whim.

He heralded his imminent demise from pancreatic cancer on Facebook, where he joined up those of us who barely knew each other but all of whom knew John. We shared our embracing of his John-ness while numbly witness his passing in a strange suspension of disembodied knowing. I mean he told us lots about the various stage-gates he passed through, but in the end, I knew little of how this passage must feel. Even after death his avatar still pops up on various FB message pages.

Maybe it was just as well that I was getting into the dance macabre required for the long goodbye on social media, for, shortly after Paul's eventual demise, an American colleague and narrative research practitioner, Bud, announced his cancer to all his many followers through Facebook. What drew me towards him in the first place was reading his narrative research into him growing up in the shadow of his CIA agent father. He informed us all that he only has about six months left to live, so he set about the task of chronicling all the various stages of his decline with a narrative inquirer's zest for authenticity. We each settled in for this sprint, only to find that the predicted death day of six months would stretch far beyond that. In the end it took him more like two years to die.

With each falsely predicted ending, we would make our farewells, only for him to be back with us. We were with him at each cliff through his vivid writing, sometimes recoiling from his next post, most times devouring it. Bud was coaching us to grieve, to mourn, to celebrate life.

If nothing else, the learning from this pair of remote goodbyes may well have attenuated me to the process of dealing with many distanced deaths, some close, many perforce far away, during the darkness the covid years. Somehow, we learned the art of expressing empathy from a distance, through satellites and screens.

Brutal Endings, 2023

My plans for my smooth passage through 2023 have been brutally interrupted by the deaths of three colleagues, one after another. Two of these friends were prodigious, transgressive writers whose work had inspired me deeply at various points in my career. Neither was much read by others, though treasured by a dedicated few. It came as a shock to me to discover that for each of them, their writing was likely to die with them. It would unbecome.

I did not make the funeral of the first writer who died, Ann, but the sense of loss was deep. She had been a close colleague of mine at the university where I first taught and researched in 2004. Her approach was highly arts-based and deeply subversive. Together we launched guerrilla learning activities under the guise of conventional offerings until the money men got wise to us. When recently re-reading my narrative doctorate, completed in 2008, with a view to publication, I was struck by how often Ann was mentioned as a deeply formative influence. Ann could mentor with a look or a sigh. Or both. I hope that her writing does not go to the grave with her.

At the funeral of my second friend to die, Keri, I asked his daughter as to his prodigious writing practice. She confirmed that writing was central to his life,
saying, 'Dad was always locked away in his study, tapping away, surrounded by a toppling pile of books.' She pointed over to the table set up for the funeral memorabilia and pointed out a picture of Keri in his study, pushing back from his desk, the same pose that I later used for the cover of his collected works.

After a meditative silence between us, she continued, 'Dad loved producing those booklets of his, loved the process of getting them beautifully bound, their contents bursting with diagrams and photos of art works. I would scold him for never charging for these, for not even wanting to commercialism his wisdom. But he never did. He just shrugged and carried on writing. And he loved coming to Bristol to speak to your CCG group.'

'I am glad to hear that we stimulated him some. It always felt like we did. He was a luminary presence, yet so humble, so present. He would never take a penny for his expenses and gave away his books freely.'

She chuckled. 'Typical Dad.'

I asked, 'so what happens to his writing now?'

"Well, we will need to clear the study at some stage soon. And his website will close in the next month or two.

On his last visit to the CCG group, Keri described me as 'the curator of curiosities.' His parting encouragement to the group, via his last email, was to 'be serious, yet playful. Be firm, but vulnerable. Be tenacious, yet willing to let go. Be curious about self, but without self-obsession. Capture the moment, but for just long enough.'

Becoming writers, Bristol, 2023.

At the CCG meeting in Bristol in October 2023, I related to the assembled group this story of the untimely death of my writerly friends, and of their lost writings. I talked of my pain at the loss both of the person and of their canon. On hearing my choked telling of this, a colleague asked, 'do these powerful feelings of loss relate to your own fears regarding your writing being gone on your death?'

I nodded in mute agreement.

She reminded me, 'Its later than we think, and that we could be taken at any time.'

Again, I nodded assent. She suggested that I appoint someone to curate my writing on my death, which seemed an excellent idea. I am thinking now of a suitable person who might outlive me. Beyond that I was prompted to act in two directions.

The first direction was to pull together Keri's writings and publish them in his honour, before they evaporated completely. The act of pulling together this Keri collection meant that I have re-read all of his coaching wisdom. This immersion has served as a pregnant reminder of how courageous his coverage of many taboos was, such as the workings of the forces of betrayal and envy that lurk beneath the surface of coaching.

The second direction that the jolt of these deaths prompted me towards was to gather my own writings from the past seventeen years into different categories, including all the phantasmagoria that sprawled out of my doctorate, with the intention of publication. This process of curating my own collected works continues as I write, with newly printed titles fall through my letterbox for proofing on an almost weekly basis. As I arrange these volumes in a teetering pile on the kitchen table, I enjoy feelings the materiality of my bound books in the hand.

To know how it is to turn an actual rustling page rather than scroll down through scraps of electronic ephemera, a page you can easily return to by simply flipping back. I begin to become anxious as to who to market these books, whom to prevail upon to harvest reviews. And then I interrupt that thought to remind myself that the purpose was to collect the books in one tangible place, not to push them on a world already saturated with word. Even so, I ask myself, if, after all, this publishing push is a vanity project, and nothing more? Was this, a preposterous bid to leave a legacy, when I had eschewed that impulse in others in the past?

Partly on the back of this ego-based doubting, I have been prompted to become the curator and editor of hitherto unpublished writers among the CCG fraternity. We have each written into our experience of becoming a coach, these pieces to be collated into an anthology, as much for our own readership and insight as to pull in a wider audience. I have become the birther of becomings. It is notable that for each of us, in our different ways - as we have committed our becomings onto the page - have noticed a degree of indivisibility between coaching and writing. Indivisible in that the sense of the parallels between the interplay of call and response between coach and client and that between reader and writer. We sense that there are similar skills and processes evident in each.

Lost in France, 2023.

The third death was of an old colleague, Irene, who decades ago moved to deepest France, never to be heard from again, but often thought of. We were nearly lovers. We were never lovers, perhaps because of existing entanglements. And, perhaps because we were both born and brought up in Glasgow where an inbred sense of Glaswegian absurdity and innate irreverence saved us from taking our mutual dance of attraction too seriously. We were seen by each other.

After forty years we accidentally rekindled our friendship, through a chance encounter on Facebook. We planned to meet at some point in the future, excited at the prospect of being face to face once more. But then the worst of interruptions occurred, when she announced that she was dying of a sudden and horrible cancer. She said, 'fear not, but I grow weaker by the day,' as she guided me through her decline via social media messages which allowed me to stay with her until she died. Her final message, I thought, was the end of the matter, and I mourned never getting out to Provence to see for myself, not just in photos, her regenerative farm and adjoining ecology school.

But that was not to be the end, for months later the metaphoric boulder was pushed sway from the mouth of her virtual tomb, in the form of my once more getting Facebook messages from her. Nonplussed, not to say spooked, I pursued the source of these messages, to discover that they were from her much younger than her husband, Francois, whom I knew of but had never met. He simply said he was sorry to disturb or shock me. But he just wanted to chat to one of her oldest friends, to maintain some kind of connection. He wanted, if possible, for both of us to take comfort in clinging to whatever wreckage of our time with Irene remained.

Months later, I was cleaning up old text messages when I fell upon the thread woven by Irene and me; the same thread that was picked up by Francois. It suddenly occurred to me that the whole nine years of message history might still be up there, for him to have read. Scrolling back, I found that it was, indeed, all still there, much of it deeply personal, including her references to their relationship, and how it was for her to have a younger man in her life, a man who was devoted to her, and to the creation of her school. I realised then that he must have known more than I ever realised about my relationship with Irene in the ancient past through this thread. Did that history have anything to do with his wanting to get in touch? The next time he texts, I shall ask.

'What did you used to do?' 2017 to now.

As I grow older, I cannot help but notice that, during casual encounters with relative strangers in a social setting, I am often asked the question, 'what did you used to do?' I do not enjoy that question, as much of what I 'used to do,' such as writing and facilitating, I am still busy doing. But at some level they are correct, in that I am no longer institutionally bound. So, when they divine that used to work at a University, they need answers to a series of successive questions that pin me more precisely to the academic noticeboard. When they ask me in. what school, and in what subject, I demure, avoiding voicing the term 'business school' and all its connotations of chrome and glass breeding grounds for hedge funders. I hesitate also on the idea of me teaching 'leadership,' as this only heads into perorations of how awful most current leadership in the world is – and inferentially how I have been wasting my time trying to teach such, without role models to point to. 'Coaching' is sort of okay as a designation but can easily digress into how much of coaching is a con, which I am somewhat inclined to agree with. In end I simply say that I worked in the field of 'learning,' my unbecoming from other smudged, fudged identities complete.

As I grow older, I find that there are ways in which I can turn memory loss to my advantage, being able to take pleasure in experiences seen repeatedly anew, through fresh eyes, "when in conversations fluency seems undiminished - the words seem to flow easily enough, as if drawn from old well but come up fresh".

Legacy.

As I get older, I hear some contemporaries growing anxious about their 'legacy', and the fact that there is increasingly little time left for them to cement their memorial to self in place. I do not share their worry that I may return from whence I came, leaving the firmament undisturbed, but then sometimes legacy finds you. Last week on the crammed London to Exeter train, I was sat beside an Exeter student and got to talk of my time teaching there, and of her passage into her third year. I spoke of some of the crazy projects my business students did, including one group who went to help the nearby Donkey Sanctuary craft a global marketing strategy. I know. Before we knew their plans grew grandiose, and a plot was hatched to bring a posse of donkeys onto campus for charity and awareness raising purposes. The backlash from this bad, really bad, as the Vice Chancellor, Dean and assorted ground staff beat a path to my rarely disturbed door to ask what in name of thunder I thought I was doing. The uproar was not the legacy. In my history uproar is commonplace. What delighted me most was to hear from the student on the train that now, every year, the donkeys come on campus, to the shared delight of all. Now that is what I call legacy.

Who am I in 2023? - Christine Oram

This latest process of enquiry started at the beginning of 2023 when work was slow, and I found myself in a period of introspection. A period of reflection mirrored and doubtless influenced by the cold, dark days which I felt much more intensely than I recall from previous years. Was this my natural hibernation state at this time of year? Or was it more than this? I was feeling unsettled, uncertain and questioning my identity. Who am I in 2023? And who do I want to be as a person, sister, partner, friend, and neighbour and in my work as a coach and consultant? What does it mean to be a carer for my increasingly frail mother as her health declines? What does it mean to support her living at home (the house where she was born and I where grew up) and the sociable, funny and supportive parent, who is now suppressed by insidious Parkinson's Disease? "Role reversal - she is in charge now," she cheerily announces to health care staff on our regular hospital visits.

These questions were doubtlessly influenced by the global economic, social and political uncertainty; the effects of which I was experiencing deeply, almost viscerally at times, heightened by my working parallel issues with most of my non-profit coaching and consulting clients, who work on in these fields.

Daniel Doherty's invitation for a February 2023 in-person meeting of the London contingent of the Critical Coaching Group was timely - I was grappling with these questions and voicing out loud in the group that I was 'decoupling' my professional and personal identities was a turning point.

Personal transitions influencing my life and work as a coach

After leaving university for my first 'real' job working in a bookshop in Barcelona, my professional identity has been at the heart of who I am; sometimes to the detriment of my 'personal' life. Career options in Spain? Continue in the bookshop. English language teacher. Cross the border to renew my tourist visa or back to the UK? Work first, everything else second.

Climbing the career ladder in international academic publishing for a decade and a half.

International travel. Pushing targets. Winning awards. Striving, striving for the next stage. Pushing boundaries and comfort zones. Spending time in five different cities in one week towards the end of the last century was no longer what I wanted.

Wanting time in the UK with my then husband, friends and family, wanting to feel grounded and tethered to people and place. Closely followed by time of disruption - personal and professional burnout. Anger and disappointment, fear of the future.

Time out to reassess - "I'm going to Australia in two weeks, come with me," a friend suggested. Three months out in Australasia, discovering mountains, beaches, new friends and travel companions, feeling the sand between my toes, learning kayaking, sleeping in a hut to the sound of the waves in a remote island, pleasures long since cultivated, embracing the opportunity to travel with my sister. Return flight from Thailand, and a Colombian street festival on the South Bank.

Drawn to the idea of voluntary work with a small charity there. "We need an interpreter for the students on an exchange with Circus Space." "What is the Spanish word for trapeze?" I thought. The start of a love affair with Colombia, the people, the language, its vibrancy, and its deep-rooted social and economic inequalities.

Five and a half years living and working in human rights and social justice in Bogota. Another shift at the age of 40 - embracing the potential to live in and understand a new culture, its language and unspoken codes, in building friendships and networks, in being othered, where opportunities and doors opened which would never have been open in my home country. Supporting my Colombian colleagues by exploiting my privilege as the tall, white, blonde European woman. I am so proud of the (tiny) role I played in a multi-dimensional social movement which contributed to the Colombian peace agreement signed in 2016 and the election of the first ever progressive President in 2022.

Family is what brought me back to the UK. European colleagues receiving phone calls and rushing back for their parents' final hours. A desire to see my nieces grow up and support my parents in their later years.

Next! A student studying an MSc at University College London. Perfect bridge between my life in Colombia and a return to life in the UK.

Next! Seven years as Director of Development at Global Witness based in London again and supporting global campaigns for environmental and social justice. Navigating my first senior leadership role with founder directors, establishing a board, negotiating shaky line management issues? Roles? Building a new senior leadership team and a development team. Coaching support - yes please!

This period of my working life was an exhilarating, emotional, adrenaline rush, the front seat rider on a roller coaster. The learning curve was steep, often out of my comfort zone, the S curve never really dropping down to the point of no recovery, before the pull of that roller coaster car jerked me upwards once more to anticipate the buzz of the fall waiting at the top. A very active social life alongside parental care responsibilities left little time for rest. I thrived.

Until I tipped over the edge and the S curve was bottoming out. Not quite into freefall. Almost. The runaway roller coaster car was stopping and starting; stuck in the tracks unable to turn. I was stuck. After a series of self-funded work / sessions? with my coach, I woke up the morning after one session knowing that I needed to leave to work independently as a consultant and train to be a coach.

Fast forward to coaching sessions in 2018 enabling the decision to leave full time employment to train as a coach and work as a consultant. Liberating, freeing, exciting, scary and many emotions in between. Intense research and attending free workshops with coach training companies filled the summer in 2019. An academic approach for a Coaching Psychology Post Graduate Diploma felt right. Preparing for a call with a potential new client today midway through writing this in March 2023, I was reminded of my early clients. My preparatory notes for initial calls were peppered with uncertainty about who I am as a coach, threaded with a desire to give the best of myself to my clients.

The pandemic was perhaps? not the ideal time to start practising as a coach. Some clients were isolated and traumatised, especially in 2020. I was completing my coaching training at the start of lockdown - trying to support clients as we navigated our way through the challenges, ways of being and thinking that were new to us all. My coaching practice was, unconsciously at the time, informed by my experience of navigating uncertainty, change and transition, working with clients who were experiencing new, sometimes traumatic, experiences like separation from loved ones. The challenges they were facing felt familiar territory to me, having lived and worked in France, Spain, Colombia and East and West Africa, where I perforce learned the resilience and self-reliance one needs to negotiate change; to adjust and adapt.

Coming full circle back to the beginning of 2023, our Critical Coaching 'becoming' research group session, overlooking Platform 9 ¾ in King's Cross Station. Feeling the excitement of meeting in person as a group. Nervousness about what to expect. The seeds were planted already; the group gave me the space to nurture the ideas and accept that my profession is no longer THE most important part of my identity. I love working as a coach and a consultant, this transition in my life has been the richest. I have given myself permission to take the time, space and flexibility to 'be' and to have lunch with friends, run, walk in the park, cook, see my mum, walk along the beach in Rye and go to the market in the middle of the day.

After almost 30 years (with a seven year break) of living in Islington, I now feel part of my community, feeling proud of my support in enabling the highly controversial Mary Wollstonecraft memorial on Newington Green, and volunteering in my local food bank. The breadth of my community is far wider than North London geography - much as I love North London! The vast, generous, daunting, and sometimes cliquey coaching community is my tribe, my colleagues, and my support network. Working as a coach has surfaced a self-understanding almost 60 years in the making; an acceptance of who I am and who I want to be. A curiosity about what is next and an appreciation that the path I am on may be squiggly, uphill as well as down, with a wobble of uncertainty when I am at the top of the roller coaster. Yet the top of the roller coaster no longer holds the thrill it did. I have uncovered a different way of living and being. Time is the greatest gift I now have for others and myself.

Coaching satisfies my intellectual curiosity, my love of meeting and of helping people, the opportunity to coach CEOs with significant training budgets as well as pro-bono work with those struggling to run their organisation on a shoestring, and cosching unemployed men and women with challenging backgrounds. Seeing them fly, achieve their dreams and find time and space as they build their resources to support themselves and their communities. My coaching continues to evolve. Always learning.

Emergence - Jo Cheesman.

My coaching journey began in Namibia.

I was on a Raleigh International leadership programme as part of the Ministry of Defence accelerated leadership scheme. For a month, we had the privilege of learning alongside the Himba tribe, building a playground to entice children to school, and assisting the Namibian Government in tracking rhino by day, and by night, counting nocturnal animals visiting a watering hole. I was sitting under the shade of the baobab trees when I first experienced being coached. The scheme leader, my coach that day, sat opposite me; her wooden chair facing mine.

I remember the air was hot and the voices distant. And I remember that as our session began, my surroundings blurred and expanded around me. It was as though boundaries were dissipating and space was filling its place. Her questions helped me inquire into my challenges, nudging insights, as she listened with curiosity. I recall the intoxicating feeling of being given time to explore what was important to me, aided by the undivided attention of my coach.

It was this seminal experience of being a client that led me to want to be a coach. It left an indelible mark. Being coached, shaped my personal and professional trajectory from that moment on. It's hard to believe that this was over 20 years ago and that the winding path of my coaching practice has led me to the transdisciplinary doctorate in professional practice (coaching) with Middlesex University.

Henri Bergson, the French philosopher, once wrote 'reality has appeared to us as a perpetual becoming'. How, then, to capture on paper my experience of becoming in my development as a coach and how I've arrived at this point in my life? I am trying to put into words something ethereal, while at the same time actively creating it. It unfolds as I journey, unending. And my journey has involved as much unbecoming as it has, becoming; as much learning to 'be', as 'coming to be'. For all that I've learnt about coaching techniques and approaches, I've had to let go of coaching techniques and approaches; to relinquish my determination to achieve a goal or outcome, to allow emergence. I am being invited to cultivate my ability to sit in the uncertainty, trusting that clarity will come, and tap into a childlike sense of experimenting and creating, to allow creativity to flourish.

Looking back, my career choices were always concerned with 'bettering', either in the corporate or public sector, mostly in large, complex organisations – management consulting, NHS, an international NGO, and the Ministry of Defence. I enjoyed the roles that brought together people, resources and issues, that created possibilities where there had been devastation. I worked on high-tempo operations determining the UK response to global humanitarian crises and international deployments and advising Ministers, all in collaboration with others – the Cabinet Office, Treasury, the FCDO.

That day in Namibia, as I experienced the impact of coaching for the first time, a realisation dawned in me of its transformative power. From then on, I purposely manoeuvred myself into positions where I could learn how to bring a coaching approach to my work. I qualified as a trainer and coach, worked on major organisational change programmes and leadership initiatives. In time, I came to support and assess others on their coaching education programmes, which propelled me forward. My ever-present purpose is reassuring in my moments of indecision; it's the light that guides me. I've always been fascinated by learning and transformation, driven by a positive social impact, curious to explore life's existential questions, and how we can collectively contribute to a better world.

I was eager for the experiential learning I needed to hone my skills. It was through the *i-coach* coaching consultancy, that I came to understand how my background, skills, beliefs and experience inform my coaching 'signature presence' – appreciating that 'who you are is how you coach'. Each of our signatures is unique, of course. Mine is a never-ending craft; at its essence, it's the same, but it shifts with each new influence, learning and encounter. I see that I learnt, and still do, through hours of dialogue with my cohort, tutors and others, hours of study, application, experimentation, supervision, and critical reflection. I created my approach from the host of coaching philosophies, methods and approaches.

As much as we learn from formal training, what I find intriguing is what happens to our learning during the in-between times. The intensity of some of these experiences for me - bringing our two children into the world, moving house many times, experiencing bereavements, coping in distressing times, the Covid pandemic – seem to have grown my strength in facing darkness, both within myself and with my clients. As a military family, we have lived with danger, uncertainty and separation, familiar with loss, grief, life-changing injuries and death. My co-coach reminds me that the answer lies in facing this discomfort, to ask what it's telling me in the silence. I have discovered that I need to work deeply on my own inner challenges to refine my skills of enquiry with others. I instinctively feel this embodied wisdom. This gives me the strength to hold the space for clients so we can inquire into the dark places and explore the paradoxes together. In that way, shifts occur.

I rely on critical reflection to build my self-awareness. It has always been an essential part of my development. Patterns emerge, insights, meaning. I seek out transitional places - hotels, art galleries, train stations - as they allow anonymity, freedom from expectations, censorship and judgement. Meditation in movement - running, stand-up paddle boarding, flow yoga - has a similar effect. Reflection is my route inwards which builds my muscles of reflexivity, enhancing my ability to be present and allowing my intuition to guide me. There's always more work for me to do. Ultimately, coaching is, for me, reflective and happens in a liminal learning space. As coaches we talk of 'holding the space' for clients - the emotional, spiritual, embodied space - contained by almost imperceptible boundaries of time, confidentiality and ethics. We co-create the conditions for change; for the emergence of something that we were not aware of at the outset, the possibility of a different way of being and relating. The moment of epiphany, of illuminating the ways to see and make sense of a situation differently, seems to me to be where the magic of coaching lies.

One of my greatest learnings lies in discovering has been how much of myself I bring to each coaching session. Early on in my practice, I remember experimenting with remaining 'objective', trying not to influence the client with my own way of being and worldview, while simultaneously conceding that I cannot and would not wish to eliminate myself from the relationship. Holding this tension without resolution, this embeddedness becomes an art form, a creative act, a dance. I've come to realise that the most profound shifts often come from those relational insights gained from interactions and exchanges as beings-in-the-world. This embedded approach calls on me to be bold and offer challenge.

My children have taught me this time and again - to embrace my purpose, to step up. I remember the moment I felt a sudden, cold liquid wave of panic wash over me as I realised that I would one day be leaving my children, all our children, in a world facing some of the greatest challenges in human history. I was gripped by an urgency to make a contribution to deeply concerning global issues where my passion lies.

Engaging in my doctorate is my way of navigating the complexity of the ever-changing landscape in which we find ourselves. I am seeking to better understand how my inquiry and research can practically benefit others, including the coaching community, to inform their work with leaders and organisations.

I am curious to explore ways that we can change climates, particularly in the areas of climate change and biodiversity loss, both collectively and individually, making systemic shifts, as much as urgent actions. Changing climates begins with me, with each of us, so that we, in turn, change the environments we encounter. My doctorate is giving me a deeper appreciation of my agency in my unique context. Humbly, I see how much I still have to learn. My decision to embrace a transdisciplinary research approach requires us to genuinely shift our paradigms, to transcend disciplinary boundaries and honour all perspectives. Our attention to language and power dynamics are key. It calls on us to have a systemic, interconnected view of the world and collaborate creatively to make a positive difference.

At times, when it feels overwhelming, I take my inspiration from the natural world and from others – coaches, clients, philosophers, thinkers, musical performers. I experience the work of musicians like Jacob Collier, who experiment collaboratively, deeply enriching my journey. All the influences converge. Becoming transdisciplinary feels like my own act of emergence.

So many have generously shared their wisdom with me on my path of becoming and unbecoming; their nurture, support and challenge is part of my story. Within my narrative, weaved with joy, are threads of gratitude. The Critical Coaching Group and its 'Becoming' Project is an eye-opening endeavour that invites all of us to be vulnerable to see what might flourish.

THREE LEGS

Three quotes from the Tempest howl, blow and permeate their way through my reflections on coaching and writing. Thinking in threes has always been handy for summarising and for remembering homework - very useful both in coaching and with fading memory. Discussions about sustainability with my young mentees who are working on creative business start-ups often weave into strong images of ropes or plaits or braids, and then there is the useful metaphor of the three-legged stool which never falls over, unlike two legged humans, who are more likely to.

My own three-legged stool is a special object kicking around my home: special because it was botched together with sailors knots by my late husband, who wasted not.

This reminds me, I haven't seen my stool recently. Probably it's been taken to the tip by my three safety conscious children, mindful of their own little kids climbing on dodgy things which are on their last legs, tied together with unravelling string. My stool's disappearance is one of many little bits of underpinning that I thought I had had around and about me, carrying meaning, laughter and tears, but now getting increasingly weightless and dissolving from view. Small things get lost, they turn into intrusive little ghosts who come to haunt you and make you gulp.

Firstly, "Our Revels Now Are Ended"

At the end of The Tempest Prospero - magician, scientist, trickster, an exiled Duke and powerful lord of the island, speaks directly to the audience before he exits the stage. The Tempest is thought to be Shakespeare's last play and is often taken as his own farewell to writing, his own unbecoming. Prospero says that he has given up his magic powers to become an ordinary human being. I am no Shakespeare expert so scholarly readers please forgive me.

Our revels now are ended
As I foretold you, were all spirits and
Are melted into air, into thin air.
And, like the baseless fabric of this vision,
The cloud-capped towers, the gorgeous palaces,
The solemn temples, the great globe itself—
Yea, all which it inherit—shall dissolve
And, like this insubstantial pageant faded,
Leave not a rack behind. We are such stuff
As dreams are made on, and our little life
Is rounded with a sleep.

Secondly, "This Rough Magic I here abjure".

Just as in in getting older, in writing as much as in coaching practice, Prospero's story is about a journey that speaks to us: full of plots, shipwrecks, cruelty and abuse, love and increasingly the primacy of nature and the non-human. There's a trajectory to reach a place and an expression of self acceptance. Prospero's self-creation and self-realisation stages (two of three phases of self-actualising to which coaches often refer in discussions), had been full of tricks and commanding behaviour. To get to phase three, he must lose his props, his trickery and his controlling infrastructure in order to become ordinary. Without his props: metaphysical, material, magical, theoretical, Prospero becomes merely an ordinary expression of life.

Our best writing, our best co-coaching is just that, it's about getting in touch with a current that works to express itself through us. It becomes an appreciation, a gratitude for the fact that we are simply here and there's nothing more and there is nothing more we need to add. Prospero renounces magic, he breaks his staff and drowns his book.

But this Rough Magic

I here abjure, and when I have required
Some heavenly music, which even now I do,
To work mine end upon their senses that
This airy charm is for, I'll break my staff,
Bury it certain fathoms in the earth,
And, deeper than did ever plummet sound,
I'll drown my book.

Being ordinary and taking pleasure in the ordinary reminds me of a book I read about George Orwell. (*Orwell's Roses by Rebecca Solnit, 2022*). Orwell loved roses and probably hollyhocks too, despite the bourgeois taint of being associated with flower gardening and in pleasure for pleasure's sake.

Thirdly, "With the Help of your Good Hands".

Prospero can't do it by himself ! Before he exits, he asks his audience to pardon the deceiver, that is to say himself, as well as to pardon the tally of his badnesses and excesses on the island (Note: Shakespeare scholars like to discuss whether Shakespeare was a Humanist – is this about human progress?). The audience is asked to set him free with their applause. "Release me from my bands with the help of your good hands".
The audience is needed to actively complete the plot and the play itself.

Take a look at a recent award winning one person show called *'Every Brilliant Thing' by Duncan Macmillan. The plot* is simple enough—a young boy decides to catalogue a list of things worth living for after his Mother's suicide attempt. The audience is given numbered cards with statements of simple pleasures like 'the colour yellow' The boy keeps the list for years and it reaches into the thousands. The play unfolds through a total sense of connection between actor and audience.

"Who or what helps you?", is a fertile question we ask together. It usually evokes a rich response.

In Prospero's final lines he asks for the audience's forgiveness for what he has done; to pardon him for his actions on the island, which he is now restoring to its natural state, without his magic. He moves from ego to eco. It's an overused phrase, but it's an apt response to The Tempest.

Now my charms are all o'erthrown,
And what strength I have's mine own,
Which is most faint:
But release me from my bands
With the help of your good hands:
Gentle breath of yours my sails
Must fill, or else my project fails,

Which was to please. Now I lack
Spirits to enforce, art to enchant,
And my ending is despair,
Unless I be relieved by prayer
………As you from crimes would pardoned be,
Let your indulgence set me free.

We learn that he'll breathe his last breaths 'free'd up '.
How often does the theme of freedom, constraint, structure
and boundary come up in coaching and in writing, and in the
tension between desire and framing?

'ONLY CONNECT – Live in Fragments No Longer' (*E.M Forster: Howards End 1910*)

We all mess up and we lose our connection to the imagination
that actually is the support to our lives. But we came to this
Earth simply to turn up and when we do, when we stop for a
moment and are present and pay attention and open our eyes
and recognise what it is we are a part of, we know there is
nothing left to say but 'thank you.' We need to step out of the
way for just a moment, and get over our egos, to just stop and
look and connect to each other.

Often, coach and client laugh together in sessions as we trawl the significant objects and stories of our lives, delighted and surprised by what they carry and contain: my broken three-legged stool, Prospero's broken staff, our lost husbands, my lost lover re-united after three score years.

In a recent coaching session with Ms X, we talked about theatre. We talked about three very useful questions to ask of a play: 1. Did I concentrate? 2. Did it make me think? 3. Did it make me feel?

Ms X told me about her son getting tickets for his Dad for his birthday to see Darren Brown's magic show in the West End. The Company made a random phone call to her son and a subterfuge plan was made for his older brother to be secreted onto the stage in a container. Unsuspectingly, Dad was to be invited onto the stage and older son was going to be revealed in a grand finale of splendid razzmatazz. What a totally Shakespearean idea! except that the brothers were not identical twins. Unfortunately, Father and younger son became increasingly bored during the first half of the show. They were far from being enchanted. They'd voted with their feet on question 1. At half time they decided that the pub was a better place for them. In vain the appointed member of the cast called out for Mr X. He was not forthcoming. The show ended, a damp squib. There was no marvelling at dark tricks, no frisson resonating with our worst fears and imaginings, just unintended cock up.

In our coaching conversation we talked about folly, we talked about sons, we talked about disappointment and loss, and along the way de-activated a couple of lurking ghosts who had been intruding.

Latterly, so many of my coaching conversations have been about the tensions between different kinds of knowledge, with different routes of accountability and with the separation and shredding of strands of knowledge in our contemporary world, leading to the unravelling of plots and braids and the conflict inherent in struggling with different priorities. This indicates a need to write for ourselves stories about connectedness, uncertainty and multiplicity to counter the increasing polarities and clashes which surround us. I hear talk about valuing different kinds of knowledge and the many different and sometimes ordinary ways of making change in our lives, recognising that some of us are connectors, some are transformers or adaptors, others are singers, dancers, story tellers and painters. Look awry, get out of your own narrative, where it's easier to show pain than love.

My client and I swap book suggestions. We look at pictures and poems and walk. It's learning by talking, it's mutual. At best, we find surprise, revelation and a sense of excitement that is similar to the process of writing in that we generate co-creative energy and confidence.

Becoming, through Courage and Resilience - Jeannette Marshall

When asked to participate in writing a short piece about 'becoming', my starting point was to look at the word's definition. Little did I realise the profound impact of this activity on the direction I decided to take. Dictionary.com explains 'becoming' as 'any change involving realisation of potentialities, as a movement from the lower level of potentiality to the higher level of actuality.'

'Becoming' is a dynamic, continuous evolution that propels individuals to transcend their boundaries and embrace new possibilities. My journey from being a part of a professional association to summoning the courage to walk away marked a pivotal moment in my life—a moment of uncertainty, vulnerability, and profound self-discovery. This article delves into the depths of this transformative experience, exploring the emotions of shame, the courage to have a voice, and the power of utilising one's experience to reshape the world through one coaching conversation at a time.

For years, I found solace and identity in being a part of a professional association. It offered a sense of belonging to a structured environment where expectations were clear, and achievements were recognised. However, within the comfort of this structured cocoon, I started feeling the stirrings of restlessness—a subtle discontent that signalled the need for change. Reflecting on precisely who and what I was becoming so that I could write this article was fundamental and caused me to do some deep soul-searching and question everything I was familiar with.

It took me a very long time to feel comfortable in my own skin, and this seemingly simple activity disrupted my inner equilibrium and set me on a stormy sea of highs and lows. The decision to walk away from the security of the professional association took work. It required a leap of faith into the unknown—a place where uncertainty prevailed, and the familiar was left behind. This bold step was met with mixed emotions—fear, excitement, and a nagging doubt that questioned the wisdom of leaving the known for the uncertain! Along with an injection of the ubiquitous 'imposter syndrome'!! As I ventured into the uncharted territories of my professional life, vulnerability became a constant companion. The fear of judgment and failure loomed large, yet it was in this vulnerability that actual growth emerged. It was okay not to have all the answers, and it was okay to stumble along the way. Recognising and embracing vulnerability became the catalyst for personal and professional transformation.

One of the most challenging aspects of my journey was the encounter with shame. There were moments when I felt too vulnerable to assert my voice to express my ideas and opinions. This shame was like a heavy anchor, holding me from fully engaging with the opportunities. It took a profound shift in perspective to understand that vulnerability is not a weakness but a source of strength.

Overcoming shame required an infusion of courage—a courage that was rooted in self-acceptance and the belief that my voice mattered. The realisation that every experience, every triumph, and every setback had contributed to a unique perspective became the driving force. Having a voice wasn't about being the loudest in the room; it was about expressing authenticity and contributing meaningfully to the discourse.

The journey from silence to having a voice was not solitary. Along the way, I encountered mentors, guides, and individuals whose wisdom and encouragement played a pivotal role. Their stories, experiences, and advice were beacons of light, guiding me through self-discovery and professional reinvention. It reinforced my belief that the right teacher will appear when a student needs a teacher. Throughout my life, this has been my experience, and in taking a leap of faith, I realised that not taking a different route would be doing a disservice to others.

Within ten days of leaving the professional association, I was approached by four individuals, unbeknownst to each other, asking why (or when) I was setting up my own organisation. As a result of these conversations, I have taken an entirely different path.

A seasoned professional in the coaching industry provided invaluable insights into the power of authenticity and vulnerability in coaching conversations. Their guidance on navigating the challenges of self-expression laid the foundation for my journey.

An advocate for change and innovation, another companion on my journey encouraged me to view uncertainty not as a threat but as an opportunity for growth. Their words became a mantra during moments of doubt, urging me to embrace the unknown with open arms.

Yet another individual, a trailblazer in reshaping coaching practices, shared their experiences of walking away from traditional structures. Their courage to forge a new path inspired me to believe in the transformative power of change.

It was clear that leveraging available technology would be instrumental in moving this from an idea to actuality. As if by magic, a provider of such technology appeared at my side precisely when they were needed.

Armed with newfound courage and a voice untethered by shame, the next phase of my journey involved utilising my accumulated experience to create a vehicle to reshape the coaching world. The amalgamation of my past experiences, both triumphs and failures, became valuable tools for connecting with others profoundly. The people and support I needed at each step materialised. Some will accompany me for part of the journey, and others, I know, will remain steadfast.

Coaching is more than a profession, in my view; it is a transformative dialogue that fosters growth, self-awareness, and positive change. Each coaching conversation is an opportunity to empower individuals to overcome challenges, tap into their potential, and navigate their own journeys of becoming. By leveraging my experiences, I discovered the ability to connect with clients on a deeper level, fostering an environment of trust and authenticity.

Growing up, I wanted to become a teacher, and as I look back, in so many unexpected and unusual ways, I have achieved that desire. I want to make coaching accessible to all individuals, empowering them to unlock their full potential and achieve their goals.

Reshaping the world through coaching conversations is not an isolated endeavour. It is a collective effort that involves creating a community of coaches, each contributing unique perspectives and experiences committed to positively impacting people's lives and fostering growth, transformation, and well-being. Rather than competition, collaboration becomes the driving force, creating a ripple effect of positive change that extends beyond individual interactions.

In the tapestry of becoming, my journey from being part of a structured environment to embracing vulnerability, finding my voice, and daring to create my own vision has been a symphony of highs and lows, challenges, and triumphs. It is a testament to the transformative power of courage, resilience, and the unwavering belief that every individual possesses the capacity for change.

As I continue to evolve, I carry with me the wisdom of mentors, the encouragement of guides, and the realisation that vulnerability is not a barrier but a bridge to authenticity. The conversations I engage in are about imparting knowledge and creating spaces for growth, self-discovery, and empowerment.

In the unfolding of becoming, my story is interwoven with countless others, creating a narrative of collective transformation. As we reshape the world, one coaching conversation at a time, I am reminded that the journey is ongoing—a perpetual state of becoming, where each step forward is an opportunity for new beginnings and limitless possibilities.

If I ever wanted to gain evidential proof of the impact of a considered question, then the question 'Who are you becoming?' would be it. The birth of the Universal Coaching Alliance can be attributed, in no small way, to that question asked of me.

Introduction to the 'Life Course of independent Coaches' Survey.

This paper is based on a survey of twenty-one highly experienced independent coaches, each with around twenty years' experience, mainly conducted in organisation contexts. In open-ended conversation, they each reflected on their professional life stages, and the factors that have influenced their passage towards mature practice. There is perforce a degree of generalisation involved in the fashioning of this collective account. On the other hand, when this account was shared with the respondents, it elicited from them a high degree of self-recognition, together with general agreement that this paper represents a defensible portrait of their life course, allowing of course for individual divergences from the general pattern.

This survey was conducted in 2005, at a time when most coaching and consulting occurred face to face. There was some evidence of remote telephone coaching when distance necessitated that, but by and large the pursuit of this independent career required being on the road, often at clients' premises. Does this survey, then, have any relevance to the life course of contemporary independent coaches living in a Zoom enabled world, where face to face consultation is more often than not optional? And before the full-scale 'professionalisation' of coaching, and all that development has freighted regarding credentialing schemes, the ascent of professional bodies and the search for common ethical standards? It would be interesting to hear perceptions as to whether such changes in the coaching landscape have materially altered the life course taken by independent coaches – or whether the essential approach towards 'endless becoming' remains the same, where 'endless becoming' indicates a capacity for anticipation of change and the need for adaptation at every career turn that transcends changes to the landscape.

The journey out.

The survey reveals that the journey towards independent practice is a fragile one, though this may not always seem to be the case in retrospect. As these independent coaches reported back on their early career steps, from the position of current attainment, some often spoke as if their journey was preordained, in line with the ever-onward, ever-upward foundation stories they tell others through their self-presentation and upbeat marketing; but when pressed further they admitted to a decidedly fragile existence in their formative years, before take-off. Other respondents, by contrast, spoke a well-grooved narrative of struggle and difficulty, a survivor before they finally broke through.

When pressed as to the meaning of the term 'independence' for them, a common connotation was made between independence and a 'feeling on the outside of things' that persisted through most of their life stages, suggesting that, wherever they had landed in life, they had not felt as though they had not fully belonged or fitted in.

They reported that this sensation of being an outsider had been apparent from the very beginning of their conscious lives, sometimes because of positioning and roles in the family, or from continual and disconcerting dislocation resulting from many early geographical and education relocations. They had to learn to adapt, to survive, from early on. These early experiences proved crucial in forming the independent practitioner that would 'eventually 'burst out of the chrysalis' and appeared confidently on the world stage at a much later date. For many of them, their position in family and family circumstances meant that they felt that they were growing up acting as a virtual small group facilitator from quite early on in our lives, as they mediated family conflicts and dramas.

Some expressed feelings of entertaining a sense of higher purpose from an early stage in their lives. This was remembered as a calling, a vocation towards a variety of roles, including formal priesthood, or a calling to medicine, to healing, or to teaching, though these formal framings of this 'vocational' impulse didn't quite seem to fit them, once they tried on the garments for size, and discovered institutional constraints. However, the discovery of independent co-creation did much to satisfy their latent calling towards serving a wider purpose in the world, contained in a more fluid social frame. Independent practice allowed that 'calling' to reach powerful expression through working in a style that could strongly influence and shape of the social frame.

Given their shared history of outsider-ness, and all the downsides of that, then it came as a surprise to many of these coaches that, in discovering a career path into independent practice, it was their detachment and outsiderness that was valued; where being an outsider was regarded a distinctive competence, for which they were well recognised and rewarded. They expressed that such external acknowledgement came as a profound relief, after years of being in roles where the shoes have not fitted, and having their difference regarded as an ill-fitting, awkward thing.

The survey revealed that the respondents had reached independent practice from a wide variety of backgrounds. These points of departure points included predicable starting points such as managerial positions - where they often claim that their inspiration to move into coaching came from an excellent experience of being coached - and from management consulting and business school backgrounds. Less orthodox origin stories included delivering personal growth offerings which began as a hobby then grew into a viable business; occupying entrepreneurial roles such as marketers or 'ecopreneurs' for innovative 'green' products, well before greening became in vogue; film making; setting up a western riding school in the USA; sports and musical coaching; the creating and running of conference centres and retreats; and involvement in the creative arts at many levels, including working with a string quartet, and managing an Irish band.

The transition from such roles to establishing fledgling independent practice varied from person to person. Many engaged in a hybrid form of working, where they blended their existing roles with as much part-time coaching and consulting that they could pick up. Others partnered with niche coaching and consulting firms for a while, and some still do, though they stressed that they needed to contract these roles tightly, to ensure their freedom to intervene within ethical boundaries was not too severely compromised. Several had landed an extensive corporate contract that allowed them to jump straight into exclusive independent practice with a degree of financial security, and an impressive story to tell. The most reported transition was that from being an internal consultant or coaching specialist to an organisation to independent practice, taking some of their previous organisational clients with them, most often on good terms, but not always.

Despite these differing start points, this inquiry revealed that these independent coaches ended up in a very similar place in relation to how they conceived themselves to be positioned in the world, not least in the freedoms that they felt they had created for themselves around their life choices. When his convergence was pointed out to them, they attributed this to the common values that they claimed to hold. The values most cited included openness to change; self-direction; a pursuit of excitement; a strong appetite for personal freedom, and a variety of beliefs that could be broadly gathered under the banner of spirituality, though several took exception to that term. Either way, it was clear that they were well versed in the 'values' lexicon and spoke to them freely.

The majority had been, or continued to be, engaged with education and learning endeavours at a variety of different levels, both formal and informal. Aligned to that educational direction, they had - with varying degrees of success - been the creators and developers of intellectual property matter, this IP often relating to these educational endeavours. The purpose of bringing such IP to market was to enable them to sell propriety tools and products that would yield them 'passive income,' as well as to spread their brand. Beyond education, their interests and passions have leaned towards involvement on several political fronts, including proselyting for fair treatment of minorities, for restoration of justice, or on environmental issues, but this political interest had rarely translated into a formal political role.

The respondents appeared to move in and out of these various roles with apparent ease. A common denominator was that in the case of each of their projects or passions, the orientation towards them had been one of 'co-creation'. This activity is characterised by the coaches (and those also working as organisation consultants) was that of working *with* their client and client systems, as opposed to imposing upon their clients' ideas and beliefs from an expert or guru positioning. Their mantra was 'start where the client is at.' This co-creative preference was nowhere better illustrated than in the names of their businesses, where the co-creative propensity manifested itself as a putative brand. These names would include Co-Development International, Meta-bridge, The Space Between, Limited Nowhere and other similar signifiers. These names spoke strongly to the notion of liminality, of betwixt and between, a shadowy area where co-creation work is realised.

A further defining characteristic included a preference for working with the 'emergent' process, where the coach proceeds with their client towards defining and addressing the challenges they face. One respondent expressed that the belief that guides this co-creative practice as 'change occurs in the crucible of relationship'. A corollary of this appetite for emergence meant that emergence was often privileged at the expense of 'completing and finishing,' though a few respondents indicated that they were getting better at seeing assignments through to completion as they grew older. One said, 'we love nothing better than being in at the start-up and early development of an idea of project, along with others. It enlivens and rejuvenates us. Seeing the thing through – well that is up to the client.'

Choosing then migrating to the independent life was shaped by a 'forcefield of factors,' between 'push' factors that were driving them away from their existing situation, contrasting with those factors that were attracting them towards this new independent identity. For example, for those with a corporate background, the forces that caused then to move away included the stifling vagaries of corporate life, coupled with the pressures to conformity that lay therein. Such practitioners speak powerfully to their strong wish was to escape the 'tightening straitjacket of performance management,' and to move away from 'the exhaustion that comes from being stereotyped within the organisation system as the outsider, the maverick, the misfit.' They commonly reported that, At some point, they had eventually reached the stage where they became tired of being demonised, of being 'cast aside,' of being 'censored,' of being 'rendered voiceless,' of being 'alienated.' As one respondent put it, 'I've had enough of all that feeling of being the awkward one. There was too much pain to bear, each time I walked into that institution, to be reminded of my difference, I needed to get away from it. I could not take the re-stimulation of feelings of unworthiness much longer'.

The countervailing 'pull' element in the forcefield concerned moving towards a scenario where they experienced a sense of freedom and autonomy, of having control over their own lives, of being in a place they have the ability to change significant aspects of their lives, without being censored for doing that. There was also evidence of the strong urge to move towards a positioning where they had room to discover their own voice, rather than feeling that they must play the role of 'institutional glove puppet.' In this process they explained that they were seeking a place in life where 'natural' or instinctive values were allowed a space to breathe and to grow strong, rather than those values being compromised or distorted by institutional culture. This movement 'towards' involved a subtle and sometimes stumbling progress towards alignment of these natural values with a growing sense of life's purpose, expressed in a context where they could earn a living.

Clearly, for each of them, this force field was finely balanced, and subject to fluctuation. It was interesting to hear about the tipping points that eventually propelled the respondents towards independence. For some this tipping point occurred around an 'interruption' to the normal course of their lives, including dramatic events such as illness (sometimes life threatening), redundancy, the break-up of a relationship, or a divorce. For others it was a conjunction of a number of these interruptions erupting simultaneously, catalysing major life transition.

There were frequent mentions of 'transformational moments', where the new direction became clear through a 'damascene moment,' when a crystallised vision of the way forward became compellingly clear. These moments occurred in situations such as personal growth events or seminars, through encounters with charismatic role-models, or when out in nature. Many could identify moments where 'synchronicity' oiled the wheels of their unfolding narratives, where I sequence of apparent coincidences shaped and defined their journey. They observed that synchronicity occurred most often when in a liminal space, or on the threshold between states; when in 'free flow,' in the 'zone,' or when life seems to be unfolding quite naturally, in the way it instinctively should, without conscious effort or agency on one's part. One quoted Jowarski, (1996) who writes of developing the capacity to usher in 'predictable miracles.'

Some reported that the decision to pursue the independent life was at times influenced by wishing to follow the example of a role model, often a mentor. There were interesting variations in the extent to which mentors were sought out, while others seemed positively resistant to this need for direction, wishing to do it their own way, particularly where mentors were imposed upon them, such as within consultancies. One reported that, 'there are mentors out there looking for apprentices to develop, and that if you were smart and you want to get onto a fast-track development process, you could do far worse than to seek out such a mentor, and to enjoy their guidance and protection.' Another reported that the inevitable downside of being adopted by a mentor was that, at an early career stage, 'you become the sorcerer's apprentice, an identity it is often difficult to extract yourself from.' Others stated that experience of a powerful mentor at an early stage is likely to make one more disposed and more able to become good mentors ourselves later in one's life.

Amid these varying accounts, it was clear that there was no typical learning path for independent coaches. For some the preference was for book learning. This preference was identified as beginning at an early age, expressed in an absolute love and reverence for books, and many retained that passion for reading, and for discussing the books, deeply into their adult lives. For others the preference was for writing over reading, as a way of making reflective sense of their world. Others would rather 'have root canal treatment than write.' All shared an appetite for 'reflective conversations, wherein co-creation occurs.'

Regarding reading preferences, major influences were emphatically not management gurus or even management writers. Indeed, there was a fair amount of disdain and scorn expressed for populist management writers, this scorn accompanied by a sense of disbelief – and no little envy - that these 'best-selling' books from the University of Heathrow could be as popular as they were. The expressed preference was instead for a whole variety of literatures, much of it philosophical and psychological. Post-modernism and social constructionism exercised much influence, while spiritual and 'new age' texts, with Carlos Castaneda earning many favourable if apologetic citations, were strongly in evidence.

While aware that many professions were emphasising the need for formalised 'continuous personal development' (CPD), there was little evidence that this cohort would wish such a formalised process, preferring instead is to 'get off the map' and to design their own way forward. Developmental navigation tended to be towards a broad vision of a desired future, with plenty of scope for grasping slender threads that may turn into strong ropes along the way, and for allowing synchronicities wheels to guide. Just as there was no preferred CPD, nor was there a stated preference for clear professional standards that they could adhere to. In this absence, they said that they typically set their own standards and guidelines, often agreed explicitly with the client, though at other times these were left implicit, and allowed to emerge.

The paradox of freedom through independence.

One common reason stated for going independent was to achieve the goal of sustainable work: life balance, where individuals had high control of their time, only to discover early on that, if it is balance one seeks, then conventional employment would be the better option. One said, 'the price of the pursuit of freedom is a high one, and there are many paradoxes surrounding independence, not least the paradox that independence can mean high dependency on just one or few customers.' As the novice independent coaches ventured further into their journey, then the less obvious paradoxes and dilemmas of the independent life compound. It became increasingly clear to each of them that the independent way of life is a fragile process, and they fully understood why there was such a high dropout rate at an early stage among those trying on the independent mantle.

When asked why it was that this highly experienced peer group remained in practice, year after year, whilst many others drop away, one answer given was that 'we seasoned independents are guided by an internal gyroscope, rather than relying upon external signposts and structures.' This inner gyroscope, it was suggested, helped maintain equilibrium, and allowed for the adjustments needed to respond in an agile fashion when faced by uncertain environments and conditions. They suggested that a prerequisite for survival was to develop a degree of malleability and adaptability, which the gyroscope allows; without permitting the indulgence of believing that there is 'an undisputed core identity to which we can cling at times of uncertainty.' Continuing this hypothesis, one quoted that, 'central to the working of this gyroscope was an awareness of personal values, and an ability to tune into these when the choice was for shape shifting, or the presentation of identity in another guise.' These values were apparent not only in what they move towards and embrace, but also in what they rejected or moved away from.

Sustaining an independent coaching career over time,

Survival over twenty years of more of independent practice invariably meant that these seasoned coaches faced times when the going was tough. They spoke to lean times, illnesses, divorces, separations of many kinds; and of various interruptions to work which threatened continuation of practice, together with associated threats to the harmony and quality of home and family life. Each had a story of when they were down, and things looked bleak. Most of these narratives were accompanied by a reciprocal story of a 'phoenix moment,' when they somehow extricated themselves from difficult, hostile circumstances, often citing the working of serendipitous forces that helped bring them back from the brink. 'It is at times like this that we look inside and seek strength and succour.'

They learned that to extract themselves from the pit, they had to learned to ask, to reach for support, even though asking for help is often the last thing a self-reliant independent person would want to do. They cited that a great deal of learning was to be had 'at the bottom of the pit,' and that those 'dark nights of the soul are part of the 'tests' of one's independence' suggesting that 'the deeper the retreat, the more powerful the return.'

They were well aware that the independent journey is transitory and can terminate at any time. They knew that there was no 'automatic inertia wheel' to keep their career going, while they were busy with something else, or earning passive income. The ephemeral nature of this life was well recognised by these experienced practitioners, who claimed to have developed a deeply internalised understanding that adaptation is necessary for survival and growth. Some reported that, as they grow older, they become more adept at transitioning, even to the extent that discontinuity, while threatening and uncomfortable, was also welcomed as an opportunity for renewal and for 'de-cluttering' at many levels. One stated that, 'at a superficial level there was the opportunity to discard artefacts or archives that have trapped them in the past. As a deeper level, there is the opportunity to challenge and perhaps leave behind habits, and mental models, ways of construing and emotionally experiencing the world, that no longer serve.' Another said, 'these transition points deliver the opportunity to review relationships, deciding who among their intimates and associates that they wish to remain in relationship with for the onward journey, and whom they do not, 'suggesting that 'this "neutral zone" is a time for shedding skins. We must learn, among all this discarding and letting go, how to acquire the wisdom to know what it is that we need to hold onto, and to know how to manifest that which we desire to move towards.'

Dealing with Burnout and mid-career transition.

Many respondents reported experiencing degrees of burnout at various stages in their careers, some early and some late, some more intensely than others, but all to some extent. One of the most quoted causes of burnout was client dependency, 'that siren voice calling from the rocks,' pleading along the lines of, 'You're the only one, you're the only one, we can't do it without you, we need you, you can't leave at this point, this would be abandonment, don't leave us, this will destroy us, come back, come back'. For several, burnout had caused premature withdrawal from our work, occurring through physical ill health or through psychological scarring that left them fearful of ever becoming that exposed and vulnerable again.

There were those who reported that they had a well attenuated sense of noticing when staleness or impending burnout was approaching – and that they had way of catching these early warning signs, through well-developed ways of knowing how to change the patterns of their life in small or in large ways, to cause 'their world to be experienced afresh, and seen anew.' Several suggested that, as time goes by, they get better at noticing when they are likely to go under, either through volume of work, or in punctured relationship, or beneath a physical habit or addiction, and that in the noticing, knowing that they needed to act to forestall that descent. By contrast there were others who reported that, time and again, they fell into addiction or fell afoul of the 'overwhelm trap' to the point, where descent became dangerously threatening. These experiences inevitably left them chastened, in those moments when they were clear that things need to be done to take preventative action against this descent occurring in the future, but not always succeeding in following these good intentions through.

By contrast, there were some who liked it when all of life's dices are thrown up at the same time, forcing them to meet many challenges simultaneously. These multiple upheavals could be caused by any combination of the personal, professional, relational or locational dimensions of their lives. Those who liked to rise to such challenges indicated that they were mostly to like to say, 'what the hell, I am an open system, all these aspects of my life are interdependent anyway, so I may as well deal with all the changes and the chaos together'. Indeed, it emerged that one person liked to throw all the dice in the air, even when their lives were looking enviably stable.

Others were far more circumspect about transition, and prefer a more cautious, planful approach.

The evidence was that, by self-report, independents tend not to wait for mid-life crises to disrupt their lives. They have come to anticipate that 'transitional challenges occur many times in life, and that, 'the more adept you become at facing these challenges, the more deeply satisfying your ensuing life will be.' One respondent mentioned the phenomenon of the 'transitional deficit' which, if it is not sorted first time around, will come around again. demanding that the debt be cleared, and the unfinished business resolved. This deficit relates to moving onto the next thing without stopping to reflect on and work through unresolved underlying issues that might have caused the need to move on in the first place. It was suggested that 'if these deficits are not worked through, then they cling like barnacles to our sides, layer upon crusty layer, hindering forward progress, as they pull us back to the past.'

Crises of faith.

Just as engagement with co-creation work has been associated with a sense of calling, then it was reported that there is also the likelihood of experiencing a 'crisis of faith' at a later stage in the pursuit of co-creation. This could occur when the going was getting rough, or at other times announcing itself as simply a matter of 'not feeling it anymore.' These crises were sometimes momentary, sometimes irreversible. It was stated that there were times when the meaning of this coaching work was deeply challenged through failures or betrayals, precipitating deep questions and painful transitional choices. For some, these crises of faith were said to have at their heart the issue of whether one was making a difference, or whether indeed had ever made difference. It was suggested that purpose driven, reflective independents have a propensity for soul-searching, and for intense agonisation, while others, coming from a different occupational culture, may might just shrug their shoulders in the face of adversity, pick up the cheque and get on with the next thing. Part of the agonisation process 'was a belief that holding a continuing sense of doubt about our practice is ethically healthy, and that without that doubt there is a real danger of disappearing into hubris, or of an already more than healthy ego inflating towards full on narcissism.' There was a shared awareness that this inner turmoil could also lead us to a paralysis of inaction that those around them found most frustrating, and whose inclination was to say, 'snap out of it, to 'get out more', or 'don't you realise how fortunate we are,' which rarely helped.

One frequently reported learned from the experience of multiple transitions was that 'time is not what we think it is ... I have grown to experience time as circular rather than linear. I have slowly learned that while everything changes in our lives and all around us, much remains the same.'

'We have grown to know that, if we miss a challenge this time around, then it is likely to re-present itself in a different form at a later stage, when we will have another chance to bite at the developmental cherry.'

Planned exits and deferred withdrawals.

Burnout offers one explanation for unplanned exits from the independent life. There were also examples given of planned exits. When asked to reflect on when they began planning to exit this business, many remembered that their earliest planning to exit occurred in their thirties, when they planned to retire at 50 years of age. (Some, at the earliest time, were disbelieving that their independent practice would ever endure.) They had made transitional plans for this early retirement, only to find that the allotted exit landmark passed without significant alteration in their life pattern. As they passed milestones such as fiftieth, or sixtieth birthdays, they continued to devise withdrawal plans, presaging some altered in financial arrangements, but not anticipating profound withdrawal from co-creative work, at least not on a permanent basis. These plans at a later life stage were more conditional and more allowing of unpredictable influences than those plans made with such confidence earlier in life.

Several reported that one reason for this conditionality was that, in some ways, this independence business became easier as you get older in some ways. Yet in other ways it doesn't, because that, just at a time when one feels most capable and most sure emotionally, intellectually and expressively - then the 'disobedient body' is less able to keep up with the frenetic schedules that are often demanded by this sense of renewed confidence and its consequence that were pulling them back on the road. Just as they felt more fluent and wiser than they had ever felt, then they were dismayed to find themselves hobbled by ageing and the process of physically slowing. They became aware that they need to find ways to deal better with personal replenishment, if they are to stay the course and in one piece. But it was commonly reported that it is not easy to devote the time necessary to allow that refreshment to occur, often because something compellingly interesting has comes up to demand their attention. Too often they failed to heed the wisdom that they so freely dispensed to clients regarding self-care and wellness.

End games and revivals

It was not uncommon, beyond the midpoint of their careers, despite coaches feeling fully up for it, that work offers moved away, for reasons that, when asked, they could not put their fingers on. This experience of work moving away was discouraging, and unsurprisingly caused each to think with increasing frequency about getting out of this business altogether. On the reverse side of the coin, it could happen that, after long periods of feeling a lone voice in the wilderness, there occurs the pleasant sensation of the world suddenly waking up to the elder coaches' competences and asking for it now. This often occurred at the turning point when the coach may have given up on the world ever paying attention to them again. There were cited examples of this from environmental work, and for activities such as scenario planning, two areas of expertise now much in demand at a time of high unpredictability and discontinuity, whereas in a previous time, such considerations were not a priority.

Disobedient bodies

Regarding physical wellbeing, a number of respondents had had near death experiences, accompanied by strong warnings from within and without to take better care, lest death intervene. They told moving stories of experiences of rehabilitation, re-entry and of dealing with the fears that attach to such traumatic physical experiences. Part of the dilemma of the recovery process is of the risks attached to premature re-entry, where 'just one last intervention' might prove to be too much, tipping them once more into destructive and self-defeating patterns.

There were reports of the experience of the moments when reminders of death came knocking, and the dislocating impact those reminders had. Increasingly, this cohort of seasoned coaches seemed to meet most frequently at the funerals of fellow travellers who have departed this life. Clearly there comes a time in life when one begins to bury one's own. It was frequently reported that, in the process of burying colleagues and fellow travellers, that the question was asked, 'What was the point of the dearly departed's life, what is the point of my life, what happened to those dreams that they dreamed, the dreams that we mostly shared? Why was she taken prematurely? How important is any of this work that seems so pressing, so important to the world, from day to day?' These experiences served as a forcible reminder of the ephemeral nature of life. 'It is later than we think it.' This awareness of the ephemeral also brought into high perspective how seriously such reflective practitioners take themselves. As one said, 'how pompous we can be. Perhaps we need to listen to the cosmic belly laughs that resound when we persist with the illusion that we are somehow in control of our lives, and even more absurd to believe that we could ever influence the destiny of the planet.'

It was frequently averred that 'acceptance of self' is crucial in successfully traversing the maturity cycle. A common statement reflected in quotes such as, 'we need to have worked through a fair degree of our social conditioning to be fully present in the moment during our interventions. This is where our values in relation to our openness to change, and our capacity to transcend self and our limiting fears comes into play.'

'There is little doubt that if we back off from our developmental edge, then we are likely to arrest our clients' development at that same point also. Self-awareness brings a capacity for self-renewal, which in turn freshens and enlivens our work.'

'It may not be eternal life that we seek, but it may be a version of aliveness in the now that allows fullest engagement at whatever age, accompanied by a wisdom that will inform us when it is time for us to move along.'

Extending the working life of independent coaches

There was ample evidence that, even in their late fifties and sixties, these coaches, well into career maturity, continue to adapt and refine their choices, often making radical step-outs from the known. For these independents, it would see that it was rarely simply a question of scaling down, or of retirement.

Instead, there were commonly quoted claims that, after years of practice of significant life transition, including relative degrees of success and failure - they have grown in their confidence and competence in navigating the unknown. Quotes supporting this claim included.

'The deeper we move into this independent journey, the more uncharted the waters. In this absence of external guides and signposts, we rely increasingly upon our internal gyroscope to inform our onward journey.'

'Central to my successful navigation is my in-touchness with my values, which in turn requires vigorous reflection and self-questioning. As I get older, these values begin to stabilise around valuing openness and adaptation, and a degree of universalism, where I value that which is above our immediate self-interest.'

However, it was clear from reports on the nature of the values themselves that there was little likelihood of stabilisation. Several stressed that their 'values journey' was not a defined progression with a fixed end point, but a continuous process of seeking a positioning where professional practice and the conduct of their personal lives were consonant with strongly held values.

'These values are a work in progress, subject as they are to refining and development.'

'This process could be compared to painting with a moving brush. There is constant oscillation.'

'The compass point swings perpetually, though in a narrower arc as time progresses. We can be seduced away from these values priorities by exciting looking projects that call us strongly, but experience says that these ventures rarely persist. In the end we are pulled back again towards our preferred priorities, often chastened, hurt and confused by the experience of inhabiting different social worlds that manifest different values systems.'

'Our development of social identity is a continuous process of becoming, and while our sometimes chameleon nature can be confusing and frustrating for others, it has proved invaluable to us in this life of perpetual adaptation.'

Implications of the survey for future generation of independent coaches.

Bearing in mind that each of these independent coaches came for a wide diversity of backgrounds, then it is remarkable that their self-reports would exhibit such convergence of factors assisting their ascent and given reasons for continuous longevity of practice. Self- reports, notoriously, valorise the narrative of the teller, but even so, this consistency of reporting would suggest that broadly similar forces were in play throughout these life courses. Similarities are detectable in the force field of push and pull factors that projected them into setting up as an independent in the first place, while common reliance on internally resourced factors such as staying aligned to values and anticipating the need for adaptation in the face of 'unknown unknowns' were consistently emphasised. The ageing process did not seem a deterrent to continued working in a demanding role. If anything, reports suggested that age brought with it a maturity of practice that meant that their appetite for the work and for continuous becoming remained undimmed, even if at times the market was moving away from them.

To return to the question as to whether independent contemporary independents would recite similar narratives with regards to their career longevity, these truths would need to be tested with those living that experience, given that the landscape has changed, and the market more commodified and more specialised, with independents carving out their own niche which they then market widely on the net, through LinkedIn, and through offering web-based coaching and development options. The speculation here is, despite these considerable assistances to going to market, that without a basis in the deeply seated values-based 'becoming' strategies of their forerunners, that newer independents setting out for the first time could be likely to crash and burn.

GOSHAWKS – MARY HUGHES

Clive and I had one of our bird conversations. So recently had red kites returned to this part of the Valley that, when one flew close overhead its tail ruddering the air, a small girl looked up at me and whispered, "It is a dragon?" Well, *Draig Goch* it may have been in its dinosaur past. It is now our National Bird. On the subject of raptors, the buzzard couple breed successfully most years, and show off the prowess of their offspring in flying and hunting lessons bold enough to alarm me when, once, they flew so low as to measure up my two kittens as snack potential. Clive pointed his face to them as they floated on the overhead waves, occasionally mewing (like kittens), bullied by crows yet making the hours of walking distance between the two sides of the Valley a matter of airy seconds. Clive is an avid bird watcher, an ex-miner who celebrates the ceasing of the mines. He sits on the front porch of his bungalow with its side-by-side brick eyebrow arches emphasising his binoculars. From February onwards, he and I make a point of watching the weird-eyed herons with their tucked in necks and trailing legs fly to and from their noisome citadel as they nourish their young that sit like weekend punks in disheveled bedrooms of nests. But the herons do not go up the mountain, though apex predators other than kites and buzzards do and I, several times, saw a peregrine falcon stoop like a mockery of fighter jets to take her prey in her yellow feet with their perfectly dainty, deadly black talons. I love to see that bird and I look with besotted eyes at every speck in the sky: Such love is rewarded by the most minuscule of thrills, imagined or not. Now, to my excitement, Clive told me that there were goshawks around encouraged (he thought) by the rat population thriving on discarded fast food and unmanaged as farmers gave up the guessing game of what to control, animal, vegetable or mineral.

Clive and I do not twitch, we simply watch, and this continues my grandmother's steady teaching about noticing plants, birds, creatures for the unexpected, addictive somatic blows of without upon within. If anything, this was my prompt, to get out and try out some thoughts that day, because it is always easier to join up thoughts if the physical mode is turned on. That and the consuming effects of an unsought conversation from a totally unexpected source which had nullified a long silence I had held and under which I was held. Out of the unexpected had come release and with it room to be alive, to have a past that was more welcoming and so freedom to be curious about myself as a protagonist rather than someone else's antagonist. The dotting quanta of time passing to tap out suggestions as a rhythm for a way forward, now. A future. And I had a choice of ways, some attractive, some more problematic but with all, the underlying sense and nonsense of my finite life's continuum. So, the grand old cliché of choosing a physical pathway just seemed a good idea. Anyway, to be outside in places where animals, vegetables and minerals just accept my coincidence with their time, is always a good idea.

All pathways around hereabouts exist. People have, and do, walk them often enough to keep them as features of habit so I set out in their grooves. I knew where I was going, but not what would happen: Destination is often illusionary, but decisions feel otherwise. So, I headed up the mountain behind the village. Sometimes stony, often thinly muddy, this decision was given emphasis by stamped imprints of rubber and plastic, metal and leather - mountain-bikes, quadbikes, motorbikes, shoes and boots. Other, cleverer tracks pitter-pattered confirming delicate contact through un-barriered skin, hair, and claw. On both sides, coniferous trees gave rhythm to the margins and frame to a beyond landscape. Sometimes beyond-not-far, a pinkly green wall about its green-ochre field, animated by sheep and jackdaws. Sometimes so-far-beyond that the warm end of the spectrum sped to distances of indigo falling to two smudged islands in a violet sea-sky scape. To my left (known from previous walks), I spied the ruins of a farm complete with chipped, pink lavatory in its crumbling *ty bach*. To my right, the bass tone of the Valley hummed deeply before turning to join its far away soprano heights hymning a soundtrack, ancient and modern. Cwm Rhondda, great redeemer, guiding pilgrims with your powerful hand. The ascent, felt through my boots, smelled of greens, blues, greys, browns - the many-hued perfume of the path.

The slopes had been planted, decades ago, with those bolt-straight pines grown in rows, each one within a measured distance of the other, intended to be felled and then resurrected as pit-props. This had necessitated the removal of farmland and heath which, in turn had necessitated the removal of temperate rainforest. Pit-props had held up underground passages, dug way beneath the friable pennant sandstone of the valley so that coal could be mined, dangerously, for huge profit. They were meant to keep folk from a permanent but untimely commitment to the land although sometimes they had failed to do this, and people had died anyway because trees aren't meant to hold danger away from them. Now, however, the pit was shut and the trees left to their ageing frailty, no need to prop up anything, not even themselves; the entropy of human economics and human memory.   Every now and then a rumble of nettles and bramble behaved like a lad's night out, unsubtle and a bit dangerous, growing in light wells where trees had fallen. Counterpointing them, legal immigrants flourished: knot weed; Himalayan balsam; rhododendron; and buddleia took comfortable, sunny path-side residences, invited there by humans who thought them grander than the locals. But the locals (according to their season and size) proudly stood their ground and orchid, coltsfoot, wood anemone and violet together with stands of rowan, hazel and ash claimed their inheritance. Also insisting on its rights and whispering about other days to the remains of a cottage it had known all its life and now lent on, an apple tree twisted and tried little buds of hope for future fruitfulness. A tale of transition from forest to farm to mine to open country, from extinct wolves and harvests to my walk in the passing moments of the present. All in the uncoloured, unclouded, but rawly acute vulnerability of a free-bodied mind.

Litter, like chatter in an auditorium, distracted me that day as it always did. Printed on top of a community of wood sorrel, a cycle wheel trough of sharp chevrons was spent speed and plastic bottles and packets lay around emptily indigestible. The earth would try to deal with the mess - and ask the small creatures that lived thereabouts to help, to make something useful of these things; but it would far rather not have to. I collected as much as I could, but it would never be enough. The energy represented by litter was anonymous, prolific and couldn't care less because it was inert. The path I followed told of growing, change and openness to resisting inertia, but to do this endlessly referenced the human context, its health, its needs, its fun, its entitlement to Nature. Here, were demands Nature serve us, clean up our shit, allow us in number to pursue our pleasures at the cost of her purpose. Our Wellness, her Duty. So here was an assumption of mountain biking and mountain picnicking, wild camping and quad biking bought with the finality of money or taken with the casualness to be but one being and nothing else, owing nothing, expecting everything.

The scent stopped me. The remains of a wood pigeon, not much more than feet and gizzards, feathers scattering around where it lay atop an empty cider bottle, deflated condom and a crunched-up tissue.   Choose, the vignette invited, which you'd rather: the slow inevitable digestion and fertilisation of life, does it fuck with your mind? Or do you choose to look away, with a mind fucked by desire to avoid? The soft grey and white feathers were a third idea; clean, bright and beautiful, indigestible but not litter, consumable by the world at leisure because not everything disappears at once. To learn to leave behind only slowly consummated beauty must make humanity consummately healthy. I noted the notion.

Turning a corner, the path straightened along a ridge's rim. This was the last tipping point of tip before gravity pulled all looseness downhill towards the river and human transport. The road and rail were there because connecting one mine to another had been the plan, the river never needed a plan because it had a purpose - to connect its water with other waters, lakes, rivers and oceans. I recalled the Rhondda and her resurrection from stinking sewer to sustaining water, but I also knew her banks to be strewn with rags of plastic and other items she has no choice but to carry. The river and the mountain, the Nature deities we worship through art, hobby and wellness agendas, our muses, but also our servants summoned to all matters of commerce and cleansing and to support our tales about not ever rotting because we fear transmutation yet long for unchanged beauty. But even feathers are life and become something else through rotting transmutation and, left alone, that can produce the beautiful. I saw self-planted deciduous trees made strong through malnourishment in thin soil roots like veins in old hands, gripping friable tip, pulling it back to stability. I saw dark pools of water in old, perpetual puddles and thought of them evaporating to clouds then falling as rain back into puddles; water finding itself again and again being itself over and over but in changing forms and dimensions. "Where a thousand cried on a mountainside" the faded letters painted in on a large, flat rock looked out towards another valley where, once, a mountain of human waste had suffocated a whole school of children sacrificed to capitalism, victims of fossil fuel, the coal-black death that still plagues us. Those deaths are haunting, the haunting decaying only slowly, like feathers - or a memory.

As I walked on, I thought of the wood pigeon. That bird had died for a reason, to be part of the sustenance that is sustainability - it had not been a life crushed under useless, volatile waste. It had reached adulthood and was very unlikely to have been murdered by one of its own and no memorial of guilty regret would ever mark its passing. It was such a neat kill that I instinctively favoured a peregrine as the perpetrator rather than, say, the messier evidence left by a fox, also the remains had been more dropped than scattered, as though from an overhead branch and on to the human mess beneath. I hoped for the peregrine to appear and prove me right; wishful thinking is always a bit player in the rational scenario. Wish suspended in thought, I enjoyed my reflections including those about waste and lives littered with it, congratulating myself on visions of recycling and how humans can't really bear to do it. Of course, I had not even acknowledged, never mind rationalised, the other vision Clive had nudged into my mind until it wrote itself actively across my thoughts like a Broadway neon sign flashing on and off with potentiality. Goshawk. I had no expectation at all, birds of prey are rare and my peregrine talisman was absent so the screen was blank. Then, out of the unexpected, unknowing, uncertain and perfectly beautiful pigeon-feather blue of the sky, in rhythm with my thoughts and just like magic made of all I can never live long enough to know, all of a sudden - two of them. High, graceful flowing lives vibrating like violin strings above the orchestra that is the land. Goshawks. I stared, my life ceasing in shock, in every respect but the dissolving, the relief, the sheer joy of liberty, the freedom of gloriously gifting nothingness with all its potency, The Great Uncertainty Principle delivering. There, in such uncertainty, lies beauty and honesty pure and powerful as is all extreme unlikelihood; to be alive rather than to expect to be alive. It is mysterious.

If I could have stopped my walk then and there well, that's what I would have done and here was the crux of my learning - in being unable to stop. I was almost at the top of a mountain; one I knew but one I could not predict and not even a thrill enough to jolt my life into another universe was going to get me away from the fact that I needed to continue: Nothing had actually ended other than a moment. I have heard that lovers often kill themselves because they cannot imagine a life completer and more perfect than with the loved one and conjoined transports of passion - Achilles and Patroclus, Romeo and Juliet, Naoise and Deirdre, Layla and Majnun - and people enact their passions like this a lot. It is permissible in our logic to deny there is anything else, to refuse to continue if the summit is all - that the uncertain is over because you now believe you know all you want to know and want nothing more and nobody else, nothing else matters. Dante puts lovers in purgatory: Is that where passion goes - because it is ultimately a greedy thing and a sin and, anyway, passion once meant suffering? The Buddha may have argued with Dante that lovers simply need to give up suffering. I, now free of some kind of passionate proscription, liked it and wanted less suffering. The Goshawks were *a* summit, not *the* summit and a summit is at the top, you can't take it with you to the bottom, the journey downwards is made possible by the route upwards, it is not a secondary thing. I wanted more. Freedom is really rather prosaic, I found I needed to continue to continue after heaven's gates had opened as they were just gates and to have more, I had to pass through them. But what happens next?

A few paces more and I was at the summit. The flattened thorn trees and cloud shapes explained that the wind was following its own ancient highway which came from the sea, now glimpsed properly, looking higher than the land, like a static tsunami. A battered gate led onto a plateau sliced from a dry, precarious pile of tip managed by run-off channels, concrete lined, steel caged and glued together with couch grass. "Beware suffocation - do not let it slide!" a thousand might well have cried on a mountain side. In the Valley a single, quiet mine chimney in its company of paused pit head wheels and shed roofs tried to point to something, but looked like an apology, a finger pointing to its own body. Looking up again and to the sea I noticed how it shone around almost half of the horizon, reflecting yet separating itself from sky, the

210

amalgam of all colours in the sun's rays and white gold where the two blended into vanishing horizon. The islands, clear and half-way to the mystery of horizon, seemed to float freely. Gaze at them and they moved fast yet never shifted at all. Beyond the old mine, ribbons of houses conga'd up three valleys, rivers tying them together at confluences where the houses thickened into towns but all diminishing in the same direction to the highest places, the Bannau, where Pen y Fan and Corn Ddu broke the horizon line, one pointed, one plateaued. A magnificent choice of other mountains beckoning and a realisation of other pathways to inhabit - another gift of choosing. So, still the continuum to be curious about and with it, logically, the end of worrying about destiny.

Up there, the larks rose and fell in their ascending song of warning about the preciousness of new life. All around me the crested, brown birds sparkled and glittered, bejeweling the place with their sun deflecting movement and their gravity-defying song. Under my boots, the stuff of diamonds flickered. Carbon, the mineral we became commercially wealthy on and the mineral we are 18.5 percent made of. If I think on it, why not exploit ourselves for 18.5 percent if we were willing to go to such effort to exploit the 2 percent of this land that is carbon? I picked up a piece of blackness imprinted with a fern leaf that had fallen, millennia before. The leaf a fossil, my body carbon, plastic waste made from the same stuff, buried children - time and substance suddenly confusing, tragic and irrelevant. But the skylarks reminded me that they and their music contained mineral, it being all in the mix. Clonking their agreement, two ravens came up over the summit and, as the sunlight became brighter, began to play in its luminescence turning and tumbling around each other in a glory of movement and grace all glowing with the incandescence of carbon. Indigo blue, emerald green and ultraviolet, the birds soaked in the light and became it. I called to the big, shining birds as they twirled like butterflies in a sunbeam and, because they were not afraid of me (and because no other person watched), I danced on the wind's uplift with them.

Wind is moving air, it engages the nose, and the exhalation of plants moves with it, nourishing the world as it breathes. Plants flavour, colour and perfume existence in their exchange of sunlight for life: I rubbed wild thyme between my fingers for its scent. It reminded me that there is a perfume to be understood; the top note may attract, but the middle note draws you in and the base note lasts and lasts and is, in the end, the truest scent of all. Plants know this and connect beneath the soil with each other, the great mycelia of reason and sense-making discourse, the wisdom that all is unknown save the beauty of perfect communication and inconsequentiality of power. This too is a perfume. Scented, I sat a comfortable while and asked the question that seemed to matter most, "What happens next?" This is what I heard:

"What happens next, and *then next and then next*? It is all uncertain, save the beauty and honesty of acuity, which is being here, anywhere, everywhere and nowhere - all at once."

No point in trying to scry the future to predict what I might do and be next but just stay with the question and let the world in to this, my walk on Earth among many walks. Other people might, again, co-opt me into their stories because they feel the lack a particular character or bit player and read me a certain way, however they can only do so because I exist - I too am a story. That is the bottom note, I exist. The joy is in its complexity, learning the ways and the skill is to pass along them in all acuity. The particles of being, the shreds of life, the numbering of days are all quanta that combine to emerge as the conditions dictate for survival and existence. I have no option save to pay attention and be as curious as ever I can be as only thus can I find meaning.

Whatever I become as a result.

Wiping mud from my legs and hair from my eyes, I decided to go home to a convention of familiarity. The vistas became close-ups and the reminders of my place in the roaring crowd shouted me back more loudly with every step. White-noisy, the river became audible enough to blur waspy trail bikes and the road growled like boredom under a mosaic of bird song. The mountain behind me had my back and so there was a forward, a forestory. Contentedly, I thought of Nan Sheppard and her mountain, 'I am not of myself but in myself. I am'.

Thus, I was unprepared as, turning the last corner of the woods, near a tiny slither of a stream, I heard the music. I forget it is always there wherever I am, but its comfort is instant, because I have always known it and it comes from nowhere and anywhere and everywhere - all at once. There is a song set to that music, in a language I cannot explain (let alone speak), about an alchemy that turns base knowings into precious possibilities as impartial and essential as the Universe.

Clive was trimming his hedge.

"Good walk?"

"Not bad, dry and no bikes in the way"

"Litter?"

"Yes, but not up top"

"So…?"

"Yes, I saw them. I saw the goshawks."

"Dda iawn! Hwyl fawr". *

* "Very good! Goodbye" Literally translated, "Well good. Great joy"

Take a Ride on the Becoming Theme Park.

The themes elaborated on below were generated at a Critical Coaching Gathering (CCG) convened in October 2023 in Bristol, following a number of such gatherings over the preceding year, following heartfelt liberation from Covid lockdowns. These themes are not exhaustive, and we fully expect them to be further refined as we proceed beyond the publication of this book. Elements of these themes are embedded through the narratives included in this collection. It comes as no surprise that these themes infuse this collection, as much as the authors have been deeply influenced by each other's contributions, both through the development of these writings and in conversations with each other.

9th October Emergent Themes

- The nature of wisdom – and how that shows up in our work.
- The search for personal truth
- The use of powerful personal accidents, ricochets, and interruptions to deepen our interventions.
- Curiosity as a driving force - nosiness
- Revealing vulnerabilities – self and clients
- Shame
- Being on the outside, becoming on the outside

- Personal origin stories, foundation stories, the weaving of narrative
- The resistance to name or categorise our practice.
- Is coaching a bullshit job – pure social construction.
- Stripped back – what is at the heart of coaching practice – that never goes away.
- Pervasive ambiguity, ambivalences, paradox, and a sense it will never be finished.
- Is this CCG group at beyond conventional coaching in our career stage?
- Is coaching as a profession moving towards peak coaching?
- Transitions – at a personal level but also at the macro level for the profession – and client perceptions of what it is – and whether it is needed.
- Writing as a sense-making practice

Each of these themes are developed further below.

Becomers are wary of having 'wisdom' attributed to them.

Becomers are well aware of the need to attend to their 'becoming,' in addition to their unbecoming, a process through which they let go of one state to allow another transitional stage, to emerge. Becomers are wary of wisdom being conferred upon them, and they certainly would never seek the wise appellation. They are well aware that being perceived as wise by one client does not necessarily mean that this manifestation of wisdom will prove true in all instances.

They are aware that aspects of their personal 'truth' shifts over time, while aspects remain constant as core beliefs. To that end, becomers stay true to the foundation story they tell, and work not to embellish that origin narrative retrospectively. Becomers are fully aware of the power of narrative as it shapes their own and their clients' worlds. They know that life stories rarely run along straight lines but are interrupted and diverted by forces from within and without. They are fully aware that individual lives are full of tensions and paradoxes, which require courage if one is to journey into unknowing. Part of the journey is to face exploring vulnerabilities and allowing their expression.

The nature of wisdom, and how that shows up in our work.

Mary Oliver reminds us that, 'I'm not trying to be wise, that's foolish.'

And so, we ask ourselves, when do pretensions towards wisdom, and self-conscious projections of wisdom, look like foolishness?

And when can foolishness serve as a proxy for wisdom? We do not need to look much further than the archetype of the jester, the magician, the clown, to understand in just how many different ways wisdom can be served.

One thing for sure is that attempts to confer wisdom upon ourselves rarely work; or, even if they work for a while, they are rarely sustainable. All too soon it is obvious to all the self-styled wise person has feet made of clay, that the emperor is manifestly unclad. We may give permission to others to be wise, we may defer to hierarchical or positional wisdom, while knowing that what we seem to be marching in lockstep with has little lasting power once the hierarchical positioning has been removed.

We know that true wisdom can be confers only by others. Wisdom it's bigger than us. It cannot be claimed by an individual. It can only be named by someone else, if indeed it is explicitly announced at all. And It can only be known when they are in receipt of it or witnessing it.

Can we consciously try to become wise? It is unlikely. Becoming wise is not a conscious or deliberate becoming. Is wisdom possessed within the person innately, and if so, is it unchangeable?

Is wisdom beyond self-consciousness, fully out of our awareness? Does it emerge through a process of assimilation? Is there some osmotic process whereby we become wise? And, once wisdom lands, does that mean we possess wisdom forever? Or can wisdom be corrupted, to be replaced by other less sanitary characteristics that none the less present themselves in the name of wisdom?

Is wisdom synonymous with ageing? In some societies wisdom is automatically conferred upon the elder; although this deference may be lip service only, doing little harm until what comes out of the elder's mouth is folly to those around them. Some coaches, as they age, promote elderhood for themselves. Titular eldership brings many problems with it.

We can of course turn to Blake to understand the price of experience; and also, perhaps to chime with his finding that wisdom his seldom a market where no one wants to buy.

The search for the personal truth or being true.

Our deliberations regarding truth centred on the question of personal truth. There is the question of being true, or being true to a sense of truthfulness if that makes any sense.

At a personal level it presents itself as a number of questions. These would include, 'what truth do I make up and stick to regardless?' Which is not quite the same thing as lying, but maybe it's close enough to the line between lying and not lying.

'So how do I stop telling 'my truth' when I know it's untrue.'

'If I'm persisting with the telling of truth that I know to be verifiably untrue, then I have to ask what are these truths protecting me from?'

'And I need to ask whether I'd be better served to move towards a process of letting go? or of retelling of a truth in a different way that better resembles my reality, and the reality of those around them.'

'I need to ask myself the question how much is the telling of my truth serving me, and how do I know it is not.'

Perhaps the answer to is that, if our truths are no longer honouring our essence, then we need to move beyond that truth; abandon it altogether or find a way to reframe it.

We may even need to make amends for the damage our untruth has inflicted.

Behind all of this lies a wish to protect what is sacred to us. To protect that part of ourselves which speaks to a sense of our humanness, it speaks to a gap or an absence. Or speaks to the recall of a distance relationship, where listening is needed. Personal truth may well reside in humanity. Truth and humanity could be different notes in a piece of music, representing the diversity of voices in the room.

Personal origin stories, foundation stories and the weaving of narrative

This process of weaving a personal origin story is almost akin to creating a word map. This map may look something like a web of connections in terms of events and relationships. The mapping pays attention to what we notice, and how the relationship between things and people are formed. In pursuit of this, then it may be best to deploy systems thinking, which helps create a sense of space speaking to our place in outer space, while relating to life experience

In the creation of our origin stories, we need to make connections between our past and current stories. We need to look at the stories behind the stories, the double narrative, and try to understand how these narratives shift over time. Storytelling and repeated storytelling can help bring to awareness this sense of shift.

There's a relationship with the reciting of personal narratives and revealing our vulnerabilities.

We need to look at what is OK and safe to share, to know what it is that we can bring up in coaching conversations and what it is not safe to do so. We need to notice what in our client work what is shaping their story. What are the thoughts and feelings revealed – and how do clients make sense through patterns of connection that lead to insight?

And there needs to be the intersection on the `Venn diagram that speaks to the relationship between stories that we tell ourselves about ourselves; stories we tell others about ourselves; and stories others tell about us, when we are out of the room.

Being on the outside becoming on the outside

To some extent all we change interventionists are on the outside. We ask ourselves questions such as,

'how does it feel to occupy the conventional and in unconventional spaces and places at the same time?'

'What tactics do we do we deploy to be outside of convention in our practice and yet to be working within the conventional session setting?'

'What do we have to draw upon to be able to manage that tension? and what anchors do we have?'
'What are the stories that support that positioning of yourself on the edge when you work at the centre of a structured world.

pervasive ambiguity, ambivalences tensions paradox and a sense that will never be finished.

There is the need in this work, in part to stay sane, to describe tensions in the work and in ourselves. To seek out transitional spaces to work the liminal, even to physically coach in transitional spaces such as train stations.

Much of our work is a dance between choice and ambiguity. We need to be OK with not knowing, patient with waiting for something to emerge.

An important part of this is to discover the tensions in play as we intervene, not only tensions in the dyad but the tensions within ourselves between unbecoming become unbecoming, between learning and unlearning.

As coaches we often occupy A liminal space which can be dark vulnerable uncertain, full of opportunities both exciting and lonely.

The resistance to being named as a 'coach' or as any other alternative designation may well be reflective of this embracing of ambiguity.

The power of powerful personal accidents, ricochets or interruptions to deepen our interventions.

'Have I become anything? And if so, has this been by intention or is life a series of accidents that we ricochet off?'

And do we in the ricochet head towards a cliff where we fall? And if so, is there at the bottom of the cliff a trampoline to rescue us or do we crash to our doom?

Taliesin – a forgotten story about a female deity?

Witch called Ceridwen - Taliesin stirred the magic cauldron of wisdom and sucked his thumb. But it's not about a witch and cauldron as wisdom has to be incubated. Wisdom arises but needs to be noticed and incubated (suck your thumb).

What we cannot assume is that our suffering will automatically make us wise. Our suffering is not immediately transferable to someone undergoing an apparently similar suffering.

Yet we do know that interruptions that have been served upon us in an unwelcome way have in the end made us stronger.

How do we work with others who are suffering interruptions? and how do we find a way to get into the flow?

And then there's the working with chance, and there is taking a chance.

Revealing vulnerabilities, our own vulnerabilities and those of our clients

There is a bravery in throwing all the balls of one's life up into the air and waiting for them to fall. For this to happen best there is a sense of wanting them to be thrown, of wanting to explore where they land, and know what is becoming in the pattern that they form.

There is little doubt that the use of imagery and dreams helps us to know this edge better. It's good to ask what it feels like at the edge of questioning. dreams can be used to inform our daily lives.

And there are times when actual stories about cliffs and discoveries can actually help metaphorise fewer tangible choices that face us.

Vulnerability is never far away and is easier to avoid it than to talk about it or to reveal it. But taking a risk of disclosure through writing, through dialogue is an important step in understanding the power of directly addressing vulnerability. The more that the coach has explored and grown comfortable with their own vulnerability, the more able they are to assist a client who is also in an approach: avoid cycle with their own vulnerability.

Shame

One part of revealing vulnerability is to reflect upon shaming experiences or actions that are disturbing either in the recent present or in the past. The need here is to explore what causes discomfort, what carries dissonance, and to begin to ask how that might be addressed.

There is a relationship between guilt and shame that needs to be unpacked.

Curiosity as a driving force and the power of nosiness

Are coaches simply nosy people who are looking to commodify the nosiness, to make a virtue out of it in their work? It is certainly true that without curiosity it is unlikely that coaches will be able to serve others and anyway.

We are all built of layers in our lives, bearing stratifications of the earth.

If you're looking for water; then if you go deep enough you will find what you're looking for.

Writing as a sense making practise

'The writing process has opened the door for me and my fear of writing about myself has been overcome.'

'Is there a need for everything to be marked confidential or can I go beyond that and put stuff out in the world?

The more we think about the ephemerality of writing we are reminded that it is all en passant.

What happens to our writing after we have died? is it simply cleared out like Keri's study?

Is death the ultimate unbecoming?

Becomers are well aware of the need to attend to their 'becoming,' in addition to their unbecoming, a process through which they let go of one state to allow another transitional stage, to emerge. Becomers are wary of wisdom being conferred upon them, and they certainly would never seek the wise appellation. They are well aware that being perceived as wise by one client does not necessarily mean that this manifestation of wisdom will prove true in all instances.

They are aware that aspects of their personal 'truth' shifts over time, while aspects remain constant as core beliefs. To that end, becomers stay true to the foundation story they tell, and work not to embellish that origin narrative retrospectively. Becomers are fully aware of the power of narrative as it shapes their own and their clients' worlds. They know that life stories rarely run along straight lines but are interrupted and diverted by forces from within and without. They are fully aware that individual lives are full of tensions and paradoxes, which require courage if one is to journey into unknowing. Part of the journey is to face exploring vulnerabilities and allowing their expression.

Printed in Great Britain
by Amazon

39543627R00129